# SEW*sensational*
# PILLOWS

# SEWsensational PILLOWS

Linda Lee

sixth&spring books

Sixth&Spring Books
233 Spring Street
New York, New York 10013

editorial director **Trisha Malcolm**

art director **Chi Ling Moy**

copy editor **Pat Harste**

illustrations **Phoebe Adams Gaughan**

graphic designer **Sheena Thomas**

intern **Susan Hoover**

photography **Jack Deutsch Studios**

book manager **Michelle Lo**

production manager **David Joinnides**

President, Sixth&Spring Books **Art Joinnides**

1 3 5 7 9 10 8 6 4 2

Manufactured in China

Library of Congress Cataloging in Publication Data

Lee, Linda, 1948-
  Sew sensational pillows / by Linda Lee.
    p. cm.
  ISBN 1-931543-56-9
  1. Pillows. 2. Cushions. 3. Borders, Ornamental
(Decorative arts) I. Title.

TT410.L42 2004
646.2'1--dc22

                              2003067344

# contents

introduction

Nothing is as simple or as satisfying to make as a pillow. It's small and manageable, it requires minimal equipment and materials, and it doesn't take much time to construct. But the impact of a great pillow is huge when accessorizing a piece of furniture or room.

Pillows are personal. You get to choose colors and fabrics that feel good and tickle your fancy. It's an opportunity to splurge on a fabric that's too expensive to use in a large piece or a chance to work with coveted scrap or vintage pieces. Most of the fun of making a pillow is in selecting the fabric, playing with the design concept, throwing the fabric around the room to see how it looks. I like to assemble a lot of fabrics in a pile on the floor to sort them in combinations. I will then stand back and observe them from a distance. It's amazing to see how they change according to what they are used with and in what proportions.

If you are new to sewing, making a pillow is like Sewing 101. You get the feel of the fabric, some calculation and stitching experience and for the most part, the construction is straightforward. For the more advanced sewer, making pillows is a creative experience, a chance to show your stuff without getting bogged down in epic projects. The fabric can dictate the outcome, or the surface of a pillow can be like an artist's canvas. Paint it, pleat it, bead it or stitch it. But whatever you do, enjoy it, use it and hand it down.

I hope you enjoy the book. I would love to know what becomes of your pillowmaking.

*Linda Lee*

pillow **basics**

All projects in this book are sewn using ½"/1.3cm seam allowances unless otherwise noted.

The preparation instructions in this book are written for use with down pillow forms. When using down or down-and-feather forms, the pillows are cut exactly the size of the form. For example, an 18"/45.5cm form requires pieces cut 18" x 18"/45.5 x 45.5cm, which includes seam allowances. When using a polyester form, cut the pieces 1"/2.5cm larger than the form.

**Knife Edge Pillow**
Sewing this simplest pillow style requires this technique which prevents "dog-eared" corners.

Start by pinning the two sections of fabric together with right sides together.

Mark a ½"/1.3cm seam allowance along all four sides of the pillow. Measure the length of a side and divide into quarters. Mark a point one-fourth of the side from each corner.

Sew the seams, tapering the seam inward at the one-fourth mark immediately preceding the corner point. The taper should be a minimum of ¼"/.6cm. The

heavier the fabric, the more exaggerated the taper. **1**

Rather than sewing a sharp point, sew a "soft point". Taper back to the original seam allowance width on the adjacent side and repeat for each corner. Generally, the excess fabric is not trimmed out of the corner. The seam allowances help to fill out the corner and soften the point.

**Box Pillow**
A box pillow is created when a band of any width is inserted between a front and a back.

With right sides together, begin sewing one edge of a band to one pillow section in the center of one side, not at a corner, and maintain the same seam allowance for all sides.

Stitch to the corner, and insert the needle into the fabric. With small trimming scissors, clip the boxing fabric perpendicular to the corner point and continue sewing the next side. Repeat for each corner. **2**

Sew the seam to join the two ends of the boxing. Press the seam open and complete the sewing of the boxing to the edge.

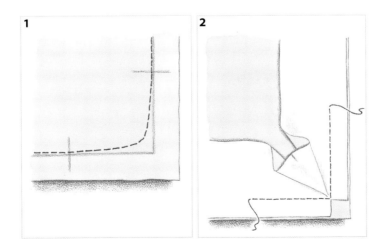

**1**    **2**

## Fabric Buying Tips

Most of the pillows in this book can be made using about ½yd/.5m of fabric.

Specific yardages are not given for each project because the pillows can be constructed in any size that works for your design situation.

When purchasing fabric to make a pillow, I usually buy at least one yard/meter. Even though it may be too much, this gives me some design options and a chance to play or make a mistake. If a fabric has a pattern, I buy at least two full repeats.

Most interior fabrics are at least 54"/137cm-wide, so you can get both the front and back of a pillow out of the width of a piece of fabric.

Mark the corner points on the opposite edge of the boxing directly in line with the corners that are sewn to the pillow. As you sew the other edge to a pillow section, make sure the marked corners are precisely in place at the corner points.

Leave an opening along one edge to insert the pillow form.

### Bolster Pillow

Cut the end circles the same diameter as the pillow form. Cut the pillow body the same length as the form. Measure the circumference of a circle along the seam allowance line and add two ½"/1.3cm seam allowances to cut the width of the pillow body.

With right sides together, sew the seam in the pillow body, leaving the ends open and an opening in the seam.

Staystitch along the seam allowance of each end. Clip to the staystitching. The smaller the circumference, the closer the clipping.

With right sides together, pin one end of the bolster body to one bolster end, allowing the fabric to spread open where clipped. Stitch the seam, keeping the staystitching inside the seam allowance. **4**

Repeat for the other end. Turn the pillow to the outside. Insert the pillow form and slipstitch the opening closed.

### Covered Piping

Strips of fabric to cover cording for piping should be cut on the true bias.

True bias can be found by folding one selvage edge of a piece of fabric 45°, creating a diagonal fold. Draw lines, usually about 2"/5cm apart for standard cording, parallel to the fold. Cut along the marked lines. **5**

To sew continuous strips together, place two strips right sides together with the ends aligned, matching the edges where the seam will be sewn. Press the seam allowance open. **6**

To make covered piping, insert a zipper foot or a cording foot on your sewing machine. Move the needle position, if needed.

Center the cable cording on the wrong side of the bias strip. Fold the strip over the cord, aligning the raw edges. Place the cord and bias under the presser foot with the cord to the left of the needle and the seam allowance to the right. Stitch close to the cord. Trim the seam allowance to an even ½"/1.3cm. **7**

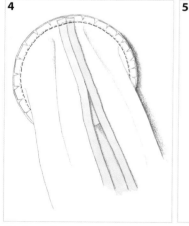

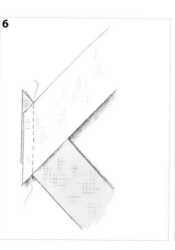

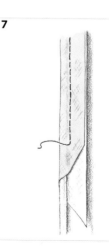

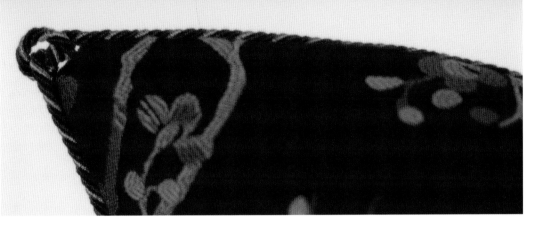

I like my corded piping to have as few seams as possible, so I purchase one yard/meter of additional fabric, either the same or contrasting, to make long strips of bias.

I am generous when buying fabric because I collect and save small pieces and scraps of all shapes and sizes. Even though they may be not be large enough to make a pillow, they come in handy for piecing, inserts, accents and edges, sometimes spurring the creative process.

To attach the covered piping, pin the piping to one edge of the pillow front. Position the piping next to the zipper foot or under the cording foot and stitch over the previous stitching. Begin sewing about 1½"/3.8cm from the end of the piping.

Using the same principle as sewing a knife edge corner, taper the placement of the piping to the inside at the corners. About 1"/2.5cm from the corner, insert the needle to hold the work in place and make three clips through the flange. Continue stitching the softened corner. **8**

Plan to join the piping in the center of a bottom edge. Leave both ends of the piping free for about 1½"/3.8cm, then overlap them and cut the excess from the finishing end about 1½"/3.8cm from beyond the starting end. Remove the stitching that secures the cord from the finishing end and cut the cord so it butts the starting end. **9**

Fold the end of the finishing end to the wrong side and place the starting end of the piping on it. Wrap the bias covering over the joint and complete the seam. **10**

### Decorative Cording

This method sews decorative trim which has a tape-like flange to an edge and ends it invisibly.

Sew the trim to the right side of the pillow front in the same manner as attaching covered piping. See illustration 8. Leave about 3"/7.5cm of extra trim at each end and leave about 1½"/3.8cm of space where the trim is not sewn to the edge. **11**

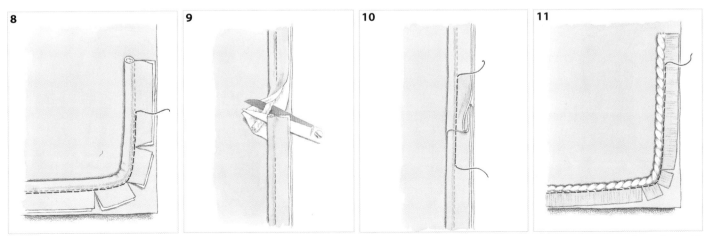

8

9

10

11

Separate the flange from the cord in the unstitched space. Carefully separate the individual strands of twisted cord and tape each end if the ends tend to fray. Overlap the ends of the loose flange and tape them together. Place the right-hand tails facing up and the left-hand tails down. **12**

Tape the left-hand tails over the taped flange, twisting the tails back into its original order. **13**

Manipulate the right-hand tails to return the individual strands to their original order, weaving them into the left-hand strands in the correct order. Tape the strands to the flange. **14**

Using a zipper foot or cording foot, stitch through all of the taped strands next to the finished cording. Trim the excess tails and remove the tape. **15**

### Ruffling Techniques

Ruffling is made easy when using a ruffler attachment specific to your sewing machine. They are expensive, but well worth the investment. By changing the settings on the ruffler and altering stitch lengths per the manufacturer's instructions, the density and spacing of the ruffles can be changed dramatically.
If a ruffler attachment is not available, this following method is a good option:

Knot one end of a strand of cordonnet or heavy cotton thread and place it over the seamline. Using a wide and

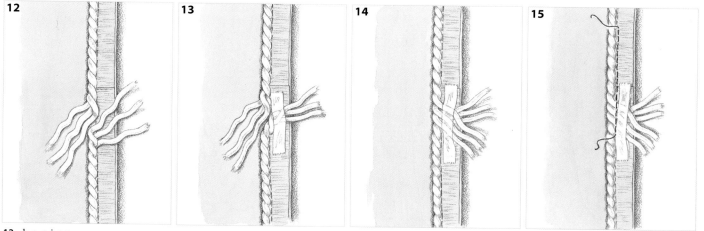

elongated zigzag setting, stitch over the cordonnet, couching it but not catching it. **16**

Wrap the knotted end of the cord around a pin to hold it in place, pull the other end of the cord and gather the fabric along the cord, evenly distributing the gathers.

### Closures

*Overlapping Closure*

An overlap is a finished opening on the back of a pillow for easy insertion of a pillow form or easy removal for cleaning. It can also be a decorative element when planned out in advance.

Divide the finished pillow back measurement in half. To one half, add 4"/10cm for an underlap. To the other half, add 1½"/3.8cm for an overlap.

To the underlap edge, turn to the wrong side ¼"/.6cm and edgestitch. To the overlap edge, turn the raw edge to the wrong side ½"/1.3cm and then another 1"/2.5cm. Stitch close to the inside folded edge.

Lay the wrong side of the overlap side over the underlap side 4"/10cm. Baste the two pieces together along the seam allowances of both sides. **17**

### Slipstitch

A slipstitch is an invisible way to enclose a pillow.

After inserting the pillow form, pin the edges together at the opening, folding the seam allowances to the inside of the pillow.

With a sewing needle and matching thread, slide the needle through the upper folded edge and at the same point pick up a thread of the under fabric. Continue in this manner, taking stitches about ¼"/.6cm apart. **18**

### Attaching a Button

To attach a sew-through button, thread a needle and knot it. Make one stitch on the right side of the fabric at the button placement. Insert the needle up through one hole in the button. Working on the right side of the fabric, make several stitches through the holes, leaving some slack in the stitches. At the last stitch, bring the needle between the fabric and the bottom of the button. Wrap the thread around the stitches several times to form a shank. Secure the thread on the right side with several small stitches close to the shank. **19**

A shank button is sewn on in the same manner, passing the needle several times through the fabric and the eye of the shank before tying off.

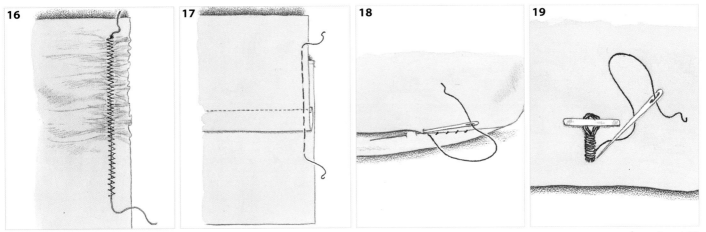

16  17  18  19

# fringes

# moss fringe

**Finished size**

18" x 18"/45.5cm x 45.5cm

**Materials**

Fabric

One skein each of 2 or more yarns

1¹⁄₂"/38mm-wide Seams Great

Coat hanger

Pattern paper

Thread

18" x 18"/45.5cm x 45.5cm down
 pillow form

*Custom-make yards of thick moss fringe on your sewing machine! Use beautiful yarns, such as wool tweed and cotton chenille, in any color combination that suits your fancy. It teams up perfectly with the heavy wool bouclé fabric used for this pillow and helps to accentuate the bold crisscrossing seams.*

### Preparation

Make a wire harp by cutting a coat hanger and shaping it into a "U" that is about 8"/20.5cm long. The distance between the two sides of the harp equals twice the finished length of the fringe. The sample harp is 2"/5cm wide.

Make paper patterns for the two shapes that form the pillow top. Cut a piece of paper 18"/45.5cm square. Draw lines from corner to corner that intersect in the center. Draw parallel lines 4$\frac{1}{2}$"/11.4cm from each edge of the square, creating an inner square. Cut out one trapezoid shape and one triangle shape and add seam allowances to all sides of the triangle and three sides of the trapezoid (not the outer edge of the pillow).

Cut 4 fabric pieces of the triangle
Cut 4 fabric pieces of the trapezoid
Cut 1 fabric piece 18" x 18"/45.5cm x 45.5cm for the back

### To make the fringe

Combine four or five strands of yarn and tie the bundle to one end of the harp. Wrap the yarn bundle around the harp so that the yarns touch or slightly overlap.

Place the wrapped harp under the presser foot. Center a strip of Seams Great on top of the yarns.

Stitch through all layers down the center of the Seams Great, leaving the needle down when stopped. At the end of the wrapping, slide the harp forward and continue wrapping the yarns. Repeat the process until you have about 2$\frac{1}{8}$ yds/2m of trim.

Remove the trim from the harp.

**Taping the ends of the yarns to one end of the wire harp helps to secure them when beginning the wrapping.**

**To assemble the pillow**

With right sides together, sew one short edge of two triangles together. Repeat for another set of two triangles. Press seams open. **1**

Sew the long edges of the combined triangles together, with right sides together and seams matching. Press seam open. Open out the square. **2**

Fold the Seams Great in half to form a flange and force all of the fringe to one side.

Pin the fringe strip to the edge of the square. Overlap the flange for about 1"/2.5cm to end.

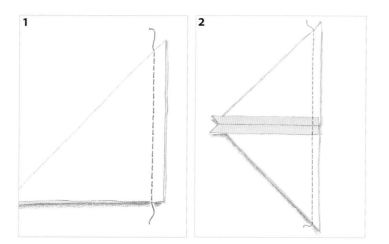

Using a zipper foot, stitch close to the fringe. Refer to Basics page 11 for attaching decorative trim. **4 & 5**

With right sides together, sew the short edge of one trapezoid to one edge of the square. Start and stop the stitching at the seamline. Repeat for the remaining three trapezoids. **6**

Sew remaining four diagonal seams, starting at the previous stitch ending points.

Sew additional fringe to the outer edge of the pillow.

With the right sides together, sew the pillow front to the back, leaving an opening along one edge.

Turn to the right side. Cut the fringe loops, then "groom" the ends.

Insert the pillow form and slipstitch the opening closed.

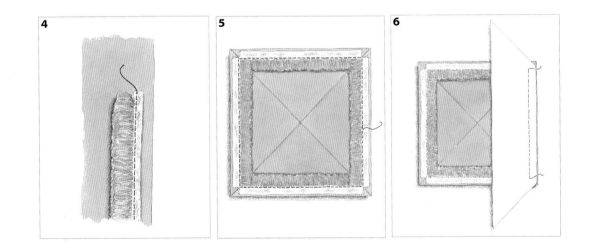

# string **fringe**

**Finished size**
8" x 16"/20.5cm x 40.5cm

**Materials**
Primary fabric
Accent fabric
Ribbon
Fine Fusing Tape
Yarn
Thread
8" x 16"/20.5cm x 40.5cm down
  pillow form

*Old meets new. Here, a lovely lumbar pillow is made from vintage kimono fabric, silk taffeta and pretty woven ribbon. Fashion your own fancy fringe using long strands of Berroco's Gláce rayon ribbon yarn.*

### Preparation
Cut 2 pieces of primary fabric 9"x 17"/22.8cm x 43cm
Cut 2 pieces of accent fabric 6½" x 9"/16.5cm x 22.8cm
Cut 4 strips of ribbon 9"/22.8cm
Cut 130 pieces of yarn 15"/38cm long

To make the ties, fold each strip in half lengthwise and press. Open out the strip and fold each raw edge to the center creaseline and press. Edgestitch each edge.

### To assemble the pillow
Press the side edges of each accent fabric to the wrong side ½"/1.3cm. Fuse a strip of Fine Fusing Tape to the pressed seam allowances on both accent fabrics. Remove the paper strips from the fusing tape and fuse the ribbon strips to the accent fabric edges.

Center the accent pieces on the primary fabric pieces and edgestitch. **1**

Sew the front pillow to the back, leaving an opening. Turn the pillow to the outside and press the ends.

### To make the fringe
Working on a pin board or a padded ironing surface, fuse ¼"/.6cm strips of Fine Fusing Tape to the top of each end. Remove the paper. **2**

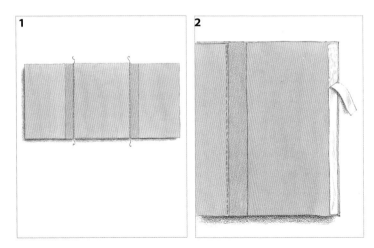

Center the yarn pieces over the fusing line and pin each end to the padded surface. Lay the yarn so that each piece is just touching the next piece. **3**

With the tip of the iron, fuse the yarns to each end of the pillow. Stitch through the center of the yarn, just catching the edge of the pillow. **4**

Remove the pins and let the yarns relax together. Trim the yarn ends to about 7"/17.5cm.

Insert the pillow form and slipstitch the opening closed.

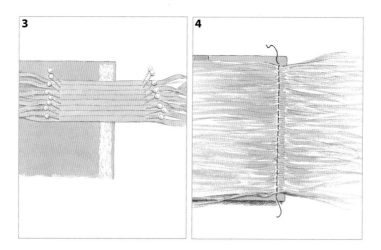

# r i b b o n
# **f r i n g e**

## Finished size
16" x 16"/40.5cm x 40.5cm

## Materials
Fabric
Ribbon
1"/25mm wide grosgrain ribbon
Thread
16" x 16"/40.5cm x 40.5cm down
   pillow form

*Contrast the knubbly texture of a raw silk homespun weave pillow with a long 'n loopy rayon ribbon fringe. It's fun to make using colorful variegated ¼"/6mm wide ribbon from Prism Custom Dyed Yarns.*

## Preparation
Cut 2 pieces fabric 16" x 16"/40.5cm x 40.5cm
Cut 2yds/2m grosgrain ribbon

### To make the fringe

Center the grosgrain ribbon under the sewing machine's presser foot. Working first from one side and then the other, crisscross, twist, fold and stack the ribbon as you simultaneously stitch down the center of the grosgrain. **1**

Fold the grosgrain in half creating a flange and forcing the ribbon loops to one side.

### Assembling the pillow

Using a zipper foot, sew the grosgrain flange to the outer edges of the pillow front. **2**

With right together, sew the pillow front to the back, leaving an opening.

Insert the pillow form and slipstitch the opening closed.

**The amount of ribbon that extends beyond each side of the stitching line is the finished width of the fringe. There is no need to be particularly neat in this process, but try to keep the density about the same.**

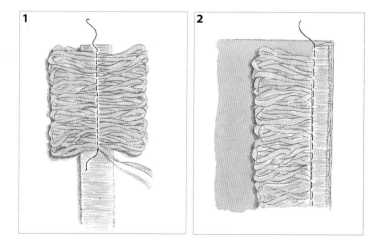

# prairie point
# **fringe**

**Finished size**

12" x 16"/30.5cm x 40.5cm

**Materials**

Fabric

3/8"/10mm-wide grosgrain ribbon

1/2 yd/.5m lengths of several
   varieties decorative ribbons

6 buttons

Paper

Thread

12" x 16"/30.5cm x 40.5cm down
   pillow form

*Be-ribboned and beautiful. Here's a delightful way to turn odds and ends of colorful decorative ribbons into fun 'n fanciful fringe. The perfect accent for the boudoir, this silk taffeta pillow also features overlapping front closure that fastens with ball buttons and prairie point ribbon button loops.*

**Preparation**

Cut 1 piece fabric 4¼" x 12"/10.8cm x 30.5cm

Cut 1 piece fabric 5½" x 12"/14cm x 30.5cm

Cut 1 piece fabric 15" x 12"/38cm x 30.5cm

Cut 1 piece fabric 12" x 12"/30.5cm x 30.5cm

Cut 2 pieces grosgrain ribbon 13"/33cm

Cut 6 pieces grosgrain ribbon 3¼"/8.3cm

Cut strips of decorative ribbons in varying lengths from 3"/7.6cm to 9"/22.8cm

**To make the fringe**

Working with lengths of various ribbons, hold one end of the ribbon with one hand. With the other hand, fold the opposite end down and at a right angle, creating a diagonal fold. Press. **1**

Fold the right-angled end down, aligning the inside ribbon edges and creating a sharp point at the top. Press. **2**

Working on a piece of paper, arrange the prairie points in an attractive design. The prairie points can be stacked, reversed and staggered in lengths ranging from 1¼"/3.2cm to 4"/10cm. Stitch the prairie points to the paper. **3**

Make six small prairie points using the ³/₈"/10mm-wide grosgrain ribbon.

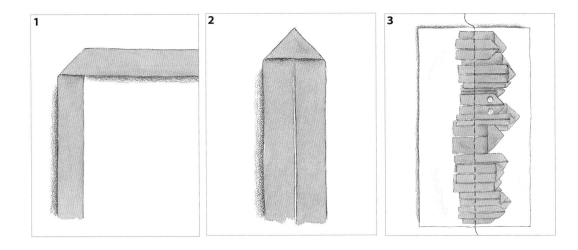

**To assemble the pillow**

Position the six grosgrain prairie points on the right side of one long edge of the 4¼"/10.7cm-wide piece of fabric, matching the ends of the prairie points to the raw edge.

Fold the 5½"/14cm-wide piece of fabric in half lengthwise with the wrong sides together. Pin over the prairie points and stitch through all layers. Press the seam away from the prairie points.

Press ½"/1.3cm to the wrong side of one 12"/30.5cm side of the remaining top piece. Make a finished hem by folding 1½"/3.8cm to the wrong side and press. Topstitch.

To form the front closure, place the grosgrain embellished side over the finished hem and baste along the seam allowances.

Position a strip of grosgrain ribbon along the seamline at each end of the pillow top. Fold each end down at a right angle to finish the ends. Baste in place. **4**

Tear away the paper from the prairie point strip. Baste the fringe to the right side of each end of the pillow, matching the ends of the prairie points to the raw edges of the fabric. **5**

With right sides together, sew the pillow top to the back around all sides.

Turn the pillow to the right side. Sew six buttons to the center of each grosgrain prairie point, through the overlap only. Insert the form.

Many polyester ribbons do not press well, so you can sew the point in place using bar tacks or decorative stitches.

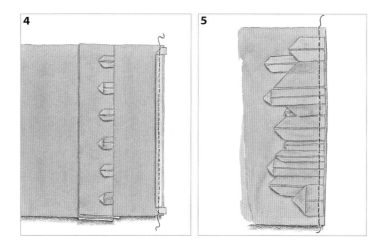

# tassels

# chinese knot
# **tassel**

**Finished size**

20" x 20"/51cm x 51cm

**Materials**

Fabric

Rug filler cotton yarn

Coordinating yarn for wrapping the
tassel ends

8 shank buttons

Thread

20" x 20"/51cm x 51cm down
pillow form

*East meets West. Here, a knife-edge pillow stitched up in an old English crewel fabric is adorned with a Chinese knot tassel in each corner. Make the tassels using a cotton rug filler yarn, then finish each elegantly with a pair of buttons.*

**Preparation**

Cut 2 pieces of fabric 20"/51cm square

Cut 8 pieces of yarn 36"/91.5cm long

**To make tassels**

Each tassel is worked with a double strand of yarn. Working on a pin board or ironing surface, anchor the middle of the yarn at point C with a pin, then make an overhand knot with yarn A. **1**

Make an overhand knot with cord B, taking the yarn through the loop in yarn A. **2**

Pull the two loops through the overhand knots. **3 & 4**

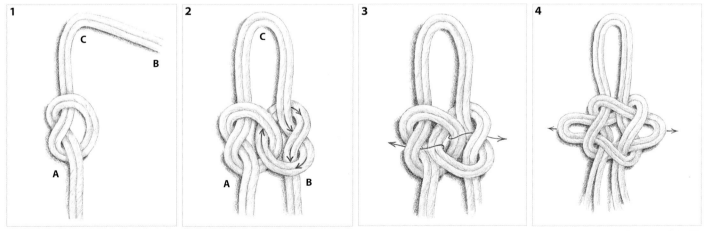

Continue pulling the loops to tighten the center knot. Place two buttons back to back in the center of the knot and hand sew through each button shank to secure the buttons to the tassel. **5**

### Assembling the pillow

Position the tassels on the right side of each corner of the pillow top with the tassel ends extending beyond the corner and leaving about ¾"/1.9cm of yarn between the knot and the pillow corner. Stitch in place. Trim the excess tassel ends.

With right sides together, sew the pillow top to the back, leaving an opening.

Insert the pillow form and slipstitch the opening closed.

Wrap some coordinating yarn around the tassel tail and conceal the ends. **6**

**While manipulating the tails, pin the yarn and knot sections to a piece of foam core board.**

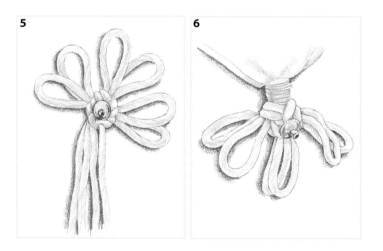

# button
# **tassel**

## Finished size

12" x 16"/30.5cm x 40.5cm

## Materials

Fabric for pillow

Contrasting fabric for cording and
  flap facing

Cable cord

Two-hole buttons

Beads

Small tassel

Beading needle

Polyester thread

12" x 16"/30.5cm x 40.5cm down
  pillow form

*Fashion an elegant envelope pillow using a handsome pre-pleated upholstery weight fabric. Accent the edge with contrasting cording and the front flap with a tassel of your own design. The tassel shown was strung using a vintage bronze metallic tassel, brass beads and jade, horn, bone, resin and natural stone buttons.*

### Preparation

Make a paper pattern for the back and flap. Draw a rectangle 12" x 16"/30.5cm x 40.5cm. To add the flap, draw a perpendicular line from the center of the rectangle up 8$\frac{1}{2}$"/21.5cm. Extend the sides up 3"/7.6cm. Draw diagonal lines connecting the sides to the top point.

Make a paper pattern for the flap facing. Trace the flap section from the above pattern and extend the sides down 2"/5cm.

Cut 1 piece of fabric using the paper pattern for the back and flap

Cut 1 piece of fabric 12$\frac{1}{2}$" x 16"/31.7cm x 30.5cm for the front

Cut 1 piece of contrasting fabric using the paper pattern for the flap facing

Make 2yds/2m of contrasting cording. See Basics pages 11-12.

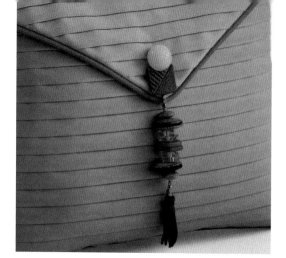

**To assemble the pillow**

Finish the top edge of the front. Turn this edge to the wrong side ½"/1.3cm and topstitch.

Starting at the bottom, sew the contrasting cording to all edges of the back and flap. **1** See Basics pages 11-12.

Finish the bottom edge of the flap facing. Turn this edge to the wrong side ½"/1.3cm and topstitch.

With right sides together, sew the front to the back and flap along the bottom and two sides. **2**

**To hide all stitching lines and for accuracy, sew on the side where you can see the previous line of stitching.**

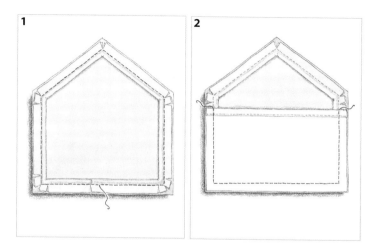

With right sides together, pin the flap facing to the flap and partially over the front. Sew the sides and top. **3**

Turn the pillow to the outside and insert the form.

**To make the tassel**
Determine the length of the tassel.

Using polyester thread and a beading needle, thread the needle through the various beads and buttons starting at the top. Take the needle through the bottom tassel and back up through the beads and buttons. Tie off at the top and leave long thread tails. **4**

Thread the tails through a regular sewing needle and hand sew the completed tassel to the pillow flap. Finish with a decorative button.

**Use pairs of buttons, stacking them with the flat and wrong sides together, to simulate whole beads. Tassels are more interesting when you combine buttons in different materials such as horn, bone, stone and semi-clear plastics in muted colors.**

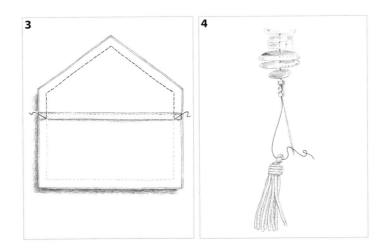

# buttonhole
## tassel

**Finished size**
14" x 14"/35.5cm x 35.5cm

**Materials**
Fabric for pillow
Lining fabric for inner pillow
4 tassels
Thread
14"/35.5cm down pillow form

*Sheer elegance begins with sheer embroidered organza. This dainty pillow has a narrow self flange and buttonholes stitched in each corner from which to hang silky tassels. Stitch the inner pillow using satiny rayon lining fabric.*

### Preparation

Cut 1 piece of fabric 13½" x 15½"/34.3cm x 39.4cm for front

Cut 1 piece of fabric 10" x 17½"/25.4cm x 44.4cm for back

Cut 1 piece of fabric 13" x 17½"/33cm x 44.4cm for back

Cut 2 pieces of lining 14" x 14"/35.5cm x 35.5cm for inner pillow

### To assemble the pillow

Prepare the pillow back with an overlap closure. See Basics page 13.

With right sides together, sew the pillow front to the back using 1"/2.5cm seam allowances. Trim out the corners of the seam allowances but do not trim the seams. **1**

Turn the pillow to the right side and stitch around the edges using a 1"/2.5cm seam allowance.

Make machine buttonholes diagonally in each corner of the flange. Loop the tassels through the buttonholes. **2**

### To assemble the inner pillow

Sew the front to the back with the right sides together, leaving an opening.

Turn the pillow to the right side. Insert the pillow form and slipstitch the opening closed.

**The tails on some tassels can be shortened by pulling them farther through the bottom of the tassel and re-gluing.**

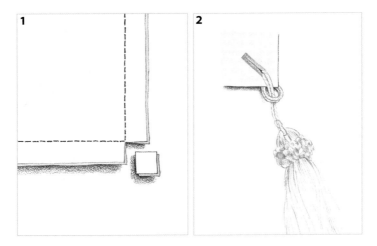

# free-hanging
## tassel

**Finished size**
18" x 18"/45.5cm x 45.5cm

**Materials**
Fabric
Decorative cording with flange
4 tassels
Thread
18"/45.5cm down pillow form

*This lovely pillow is made in a subtle tone-on-tone damask fabric and is edged with a coordinating decorative trim. Form corner loops for tassels as you stitch the trim to the pillow front.*

### Preparation
Cut 2 pieces of fabric 18" x 18"/45.5cm x 45.5cm
Cut 2⅛yds/2m cording

### To assemble the pillow
Starting in the middle of one edge of the pillow front, begin sewing the cording to the pillow. See Basics page 11. About 1"/2.5cm from the first corner, insert the needle into the fabric and trim the flange away from the decorative cord for at least 1"/2.5cm.

Continue to sew around the corner, sewing only through the pillow for about 1"/2.5cm, and then picking up the flange again after turning the corner. **1**

Repeat for each corner. See Basics page 12 to end the cording.

Sew the pillow front to the back, leaving an opening for turning, but completely sewing through all of the corners.

Turn the pillow to the right side. Loop the tassels through the opening between the pillow and the cording at each corner. **2**

Insert the pillow form. Slipstitch the opening closed.

**When sewing the corners, push the cording out of way and exaggerate rounding the corners.**

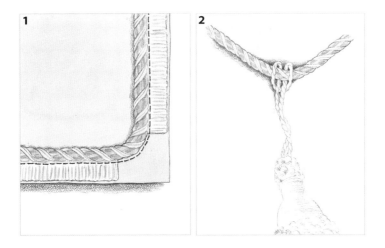

# medallion
# **tassel**

**Finished size**

16" x 16"/40.5cm x 40.5cm

**Materials**

Fabric for the pillow

Contrasting fabric for cording

3 metal medallions

3 small buttons or beads

3 metal rings

3 tassels

Narrow ribbon

Thread

16"/40.5cm down pillow form

*Three simple tassels attached to small brass rings and floral medallions adorn the center panel of this opulent Italian embroidered iridescent taffeta pillow. Covered cording in a pinstripe silk finishes the edges perfectly.*

**Metal findings such as rings and medallions can be found as pieces and parts of inexpensive and old jewelry or in bead stores.**

### Preparation
Cut 2 pieces fabric 16" x 16"/45.5cm x 45.5cm
Make 2yds/2m covered cording. See Basics page 10.
Cut 3 lengths of ribbon 2"/5cm long

### To assemble the tassels
Slip the tassel loop through a metal ring. **1**

Thread a piece of ribbon through the medallion to attach the ring. **2**

Hand sew the ribbon together on the back side of the medallion. **3**

Position the tassels on the right side of the pillow front. Sew a button or bead on top of each medallion and through the pillow front at the same time. **4**

### To assemble the pillow
Sew the covered cording to the outer edges of the pillow front. See Basics page 11.

Sew the pillow front to the back, leaving an opening.

Turn the pillow to the right side. Insert the pillow form and slipstitch the opening closed.

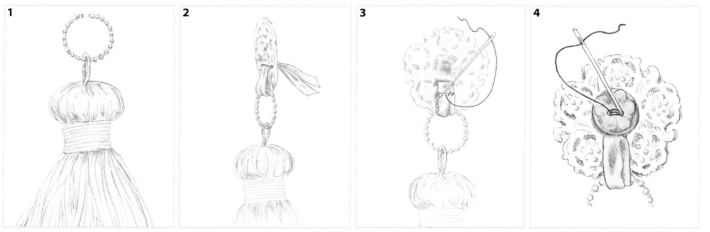

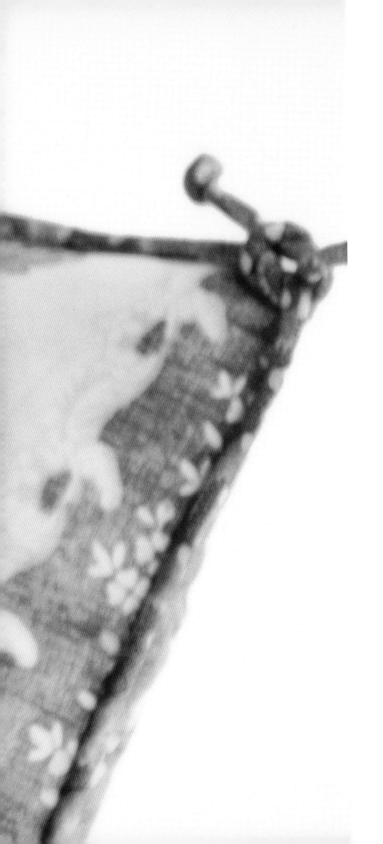

# cording

# novelty
# **c o r d i n g**

**Finished size**

15" x 15"/38cm x 38cm

**Materials**

Fabric

5 or more varieties of yarn and
    decorative thread

Seams Great

Spinster

Thread

15" x 15"/38cm x 38cm down
    pillow form

*Trim a simple cotton velvet pillow with richly textured twisted rope cording you make yourself. Choose five or more gorgeous novelty yarns such as a variety of eyelash and rayon ribbon yarns, shown here, or consider some pretty chenilles and bouclés. Add a tassel to each corner for an extra splash of color.*

### Preparation

Cut 2 pieces of fabric 15" x 15"/38cm x 38cm
Cut 10yds/9.25m pieces of 5 or more yarns or threads for the rope
Cut 4 groups of 5 or 6 yarns or threads 15"/38cm long for the tassels
Cut 2yds/2m of Seams Great

### To make the rope

Combine a group of five or more yarns and tie a knot at one end to form a loop. Place the loop on the Spinster hook. Tie the other end to a stationary item such as a doorknob or have someone hold the ends.

Turn the handle of the Spinster to twist the yarns firmly together. **1**

Keeping the cord stretched, remove it from the Spinster hook and place a pencil through the loop. Walk the pencil end back to the end attached to the doorknob and allow the two cords to twist together to form one cord. **2 & 3**

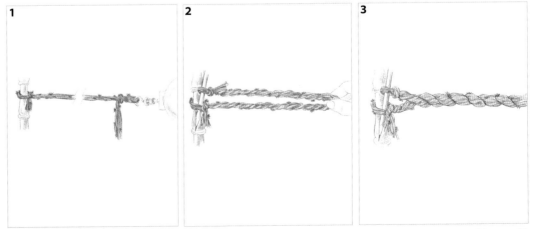

Lay the twisted cord on a piece of Seams Great. Attach the rope to the Seams Great by stitching down the center using a machine blindhem-stitch. **4**

Fold the Seams Great flange in half to form a flange.

**To get a solid and durable cord, it is important to twist the cords together tightly, almost to the point when they want to twist back on themselves automatically.**

### To assemble the pillow

Pin the rope trim to the outer edges of the pillow front. Overlap the flange to join the ends. To end the rope, blend the yarns together and turn into the seam allowance. Trim away the Seams Great for about 1"/2.5cm at the corners

Gather the 15"/38cm strands of yarns and threads. Wrap the group around the rope at each corner with the tails towards the center of the pillow. Pin in place to keep the yarns taut against the trim.

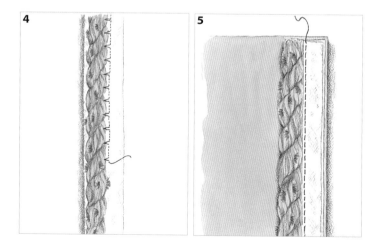

Using a cording foot or zipper foot, stitch the rope to the outside edges of the pillow front. **5**  See Basics pages 11-12.

Sew the pillow front to the back, leaving an opening.

Tie the tassel tails into a knot. Trim the tassel ends evenly.

Insert the pillow form and slipstitch the opening closed.

# knotted
# **corner**

**Finished size**
16" x 16"/40.5cm x 40.5cm

**Materials**
Fabric
Decorative cording with a flange
Thread
16" x 16"/40.5cm x 40.5cm down
 pillow form

*It's the little details that can make a big difference. Here a multi-color decorative cording is knotted at
each corner as it is stitched to the pillow front. The knots and the cord color complement the cherry blossom
tapestry fabric exquisitely.*

**Preparation**
Cut 2 pieces of fabric 16" x 16"/40.5cm x 40.5cm
Cut 2¹/₂yds/2.3m decorative cording

**To assemble the pillow**

Starting in the middle of one edge, begin sewing the decorative cording to the pillow front. See Basics page 11. Stop stitching about 1¼"/3cm from the end of the pillow. **1**

Trim about 3"/7.6cm of the flange away from the cording. This distance will vary with the size of the cording. Tie a square knot.

Position the flange on the adjacent edge and continue stitching through the corner and onto the next flange. **2**

Repeat at all corners. See Basics page 12 to end the cording.

**When sewing the corner, push the knot away from the corner with your fingers in order to sew an exaggerated rounded corner.**

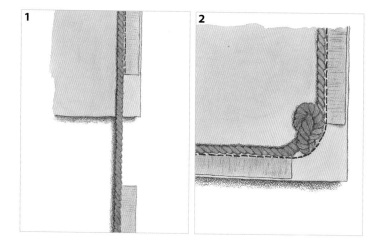

With right sides together, sew the pillow front to the back, leaving an opening, but completely sewing through the corners.

Insert the pillow form and slipstitch the opening closed.

# knotted **tail**

**Finished size**

14" x 18"/35.5cm x 45.5cm

**Materials**

Fabric for pillow

Fabric for cording

Cotton cable cord

Monofilament invisible thread

Thread

14" x 18"/35.5cm x 45.5cm down
  pillow form

*Frame a lovely linen toile pillow with covered cording you made yourself using a coordinating cotton print. Simply sew separate lengths to the outer edge, then knot at each corner for an extra-special touch.*

**Preparation**

Cut 1 piece of fabric 14" x 18"/35.5cm x 45.5cm for front

Cut 1 piece of fabric 8¹/₂" x 18"/21.5cm x 45.5cm for back

Cut 1 piece of fabric 11" x 18"/28cm x 45.5cm for back

Cut 4 strips of bias fabric 2"/5cm wide by 1yd/1m. See Basics page 10.

Cut 4 pieces of cotton cable cord 2yds/2m each

### To assemble the pillow

Make an overlapping closure on the pillow back. See Basics page 11.

With right sides together, sew the pillow front to the back. Curve the corners and trim the seam allowances through the curves very close. Turn the pillow to the right side and press the outer edges.

### To make the cording

Starting in the middle of one piece of cotton cable cord, wrap one piece of bias fabric around the cord with the right side to the inside. Sew across the cord to anchor the fabric. Using a cording foot or zipper foot, stitch the fabric along the cord to encase it. Trim the seam to $^1/_8$"/.3cm. **1**

**To get crisp pressed edges, first press the seam allowances open over a point presser. Then the well of the seam will be easy to find so that the edges press flat.**

**1**

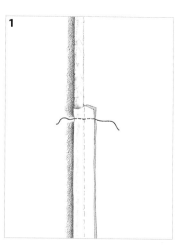

Turn the bias strip right side out over the cord. Start by easing the bias gently over itself toward the exposed cord. **2**

Once the bias strip turns over the crosswise seam, hold the cord extending from the open end of the bias strip firmly in one hand and with your other hand, continue to ease the bias strip over itself. Cut the excess cord. **3**

Center a cording tube along one edge of the pillow. Reverse the blindhem stitch on the sewing machine. Using monofilament invisible thread and a blindhem presser foot, stitch the tubing to the edge of the pillow. Start and stop stitching about 1"/2.5cm from each end. **4**

Repeat on all edges.

Tie square knots at each corner. Pull back the covering at each end of the tubing and trim ³/₄"/1.9cm of the filler. Tie knots at each end, concealing the raw edges within the knots. **5**

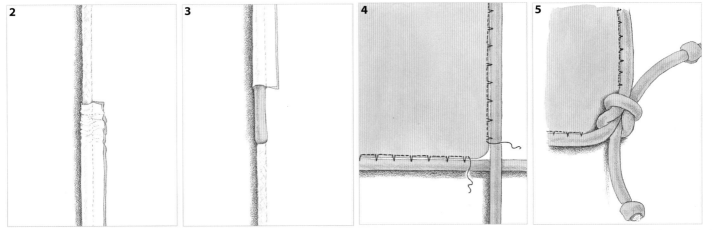

# ruffles

# stacked **ruffle**

**Finished size**
18" x 18"/45.5cm x 45.5cm

**Materials**
Fabric for pillow
Fabrics for ruffles
Thread
18" x 18"/45.5cm x 45.5cm
 down pillow form

*Stacked ruffles give you the opportunity to double your color trim options. Here, two contrasting silk dupioni solids complement the floral motifs of the embroidered tone-on-tone silk stripe fabric.*

**Preparation**

Cut 2 pieces of fabric 18" x 18"/45.5cm x 45.5cm for the pillow

Cut pieces of fabric 2½"/6.3cm wide to make a strip 5yds/4.6m long

Cut pieces of fabric 5"/12.7cm wide to make 5yds/4.6m long

**To make the ruffles**

With right sides together, sew the strips of fabric together end to end to make one long strip of 2½"/6.3cm wide and one long strip of 5"/12.7cm wide. Press the seams open.

Fold each strip in half lengthwise and baste ½"/1.3cm from the raw edges. Do not press the edges so they remain soft.

Ruffle each strip. See Basics pages 12-13.

**To assemble the pillow**

Pin the narrow ruffle to the pillow front. Clip the seam allowance at each corner to ease the turn. Determine the length needed to go around the pillow. Remove the ruffle and seam the end with the right sides together. Press the seam open. Re-pin the ruffle to the pillow and baste. **1**

Ruffles should be a minimum of double fullness and are even more beautiful when they are 2½ times the fullness. Measure the perimeter of the pillow, multiply by 2 or 2½ and add a few inches. They can be cut on the bias or the straight of grain.

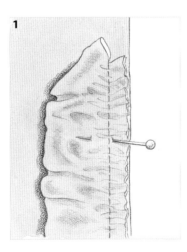

**Using a crisp fabric such as silk dupioni keeps the ruffles nicely gathered and apt to stay in place.**

Pin the wider ruffle to the pillow front over the narrow ruffle. Repeat the above steps to join the ends. Stitch the ruffles to the pillow. **2**

Sew the pillow front to the back, leaving an opening.

Turn the pillow to the right side. Insert the pillow form and slipstitch the opening closed.

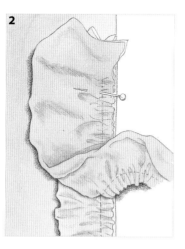

# bound **edge**

## Finished size
18" x 18"/45.5cm x 45.5cm

## Materials
Fabric for pillow and ruffle
Fabric for ruffle trim
Thread
18" x 18"/45.5cm x 45.5cm down
pillow form

*Frame a faded floral cotton pillow with a frilly matching ruffle. The ruffle is trimmed in a cotton flannel check, made to look like a binding, but simplified in its construction.*

### Preparation
Cut 2 pieces of fabric 18" x 18"/45.5cm x 45.5cm for pillow
Cut strips of fabric 3$\frac{1}{2}$"/8.9cm wide to make 2 strips 5yds/4.6m long for ruffle
Cut strips of fabric 2"/5cm wide to make 5yds/4.6m for ruffle trim

### To make the ruffle
With right sides together, sew the ruffle strips together end to end to make two long strips 3$\frac{1}{2}$"/8.9cm wide.

With right sides together, sew the ruffle trim strips together end to end to make one long strip 2"/5cm wide.

With wrong sides together, fold the ruffle trim strip in half lengthwise and press.

**Ease the ruffle closer together when rounding the corners to make the corner gathering look fuller.**

Baste the ruffle trim to the right side of one ruffle strip. **1**

With right sides together, sew the two ruffle strips together, sandwiching the ruffle trim. **2**

Press the ruffles away from the trim. Baste the raw edges together.

Ruffle the strip. See Basics pages 12-13.

### To assemble the pillow

Pin the ruffle to the pillow front. Clip the seam allowance at each corner to ease the turn. Determine the length needed to go around the pillow. Remove the ruffle and seam the end with the right sides together. Press the seam open. Re-pin the ruffle to the pillow and baste. **3**

Sew the pillow front to the back, leaving an opening.

Turn the pillow to the right side. Insert the pillow form and slipstitch the opening closed.

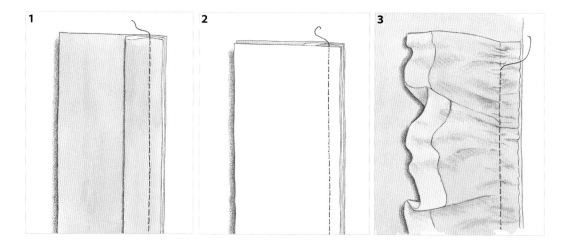

# quick **serge**

**Finished size**

12" x 16"/30.5cm x 40.5cm

**Materials**

Fabric for pillow

Coordinating fabric for ruffle

Rayon decorative thread

Thread

12" x 16"/30.5cm x 40.5cm down
  pillow form

*Go country casual with brushed cotton fabrics. Use a stripe for this elegant pillow and a coordinating plaid for the ruffle. Finish the edge of the ruffle with a serger rolled hem using rayon decorative thread.*

### Preparation

Cut 2 pieces of fabric 12" x 16"/30.5cm x 40.5cm for the pillow

Cut pieces 2"/5cm wide to make a strip 3yds/2.75m long for the ruffle

Set the serger to a rolled hem setting

### To make the ruffle

Sew the ruffle strips together end to end using a French seam. With wrong sides together, sew a $1/4$"/6cm seam. Trim the seam to $1/8$"/.3cm. With right sides together, crease along the stitched seam and sew a $1/4$"/6cm seam.

Working on the right side of the fabric and using rayon decorative thread, serge finish one long edge of the ruffle with a rolled hem. Trim the ruffle to an even $1^3/_4$"/4.5cm.

Ruffle the serged strip of fabric along the unfinished edge. **1** See Basics pages 12-13.

**If you do not have a serger, make a fine baby hem on your sewing machine.**

**To assemble the pillow**

Pin the ruffle to the front of the pillow. Clip the seam allowance at each corner to ease the turn. Determine the length to go around the pillow. Remove the ruffle and join the ends using a French seam. Re-pin the ruffle to the pillow and baste.

Sew the pillow front to the back, leaving an opening.

Turn the pillow to the right side. Insert the pillow form and slipstitch the opening closed.

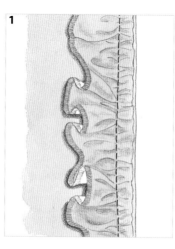

1

# surface
# ruffle **with**
# cording

**Finished size**
12" x 16"/30.5cm x 40.5cm

**Materials**
Fabric
Decorative cording
Thread
12" x 16"/30.5cm x 40.5cm down
   pillow form

*Trim a simple pillowcase with a super frilly ruffle, then add a decorative cording to hide the sewing line.*
*For best results, chose a lightweight fabric like the tissue weight floral silk, shown here.*

**Preparation**
Cut 2 pieces of fabric 12" x 20$\frac{1}{2}$"/30.5cm x 52cm for the pillow
Cut 1 piece of fabric 5"/12.7cm wide and 36"/91.5cm long for the ruffle
Cut 1 piece of cord 28"/71cm

**To assemble the pillow**
With right sides together, sew the front and back together along three sides, leaving one short end open. Finish
the seam allowances.

Turn $\frac{1}{2}$"/1.3cm of the open end to the wrong side and press. Turn another 1"/2.5cm to the wrong side and press
to form a 1"/2.5cm finished hem. Topstitch.

### To make the ruffle

Staystitch ⅛"/.3m from the raw edge on both long edges of the ruffle. Using the stitching line as a guide, fold the fabric to the wrong side twice to make a ⅛"/.3cm finished hem. Edgestitch the hem. **1**

Ruffle the hemmed strip of fabric 1"/2.5cm from one long edge.

### To assemble the pillow

Draw a chalk line 2½"/6.3cm from the finished open end of the front and back of the pillow.

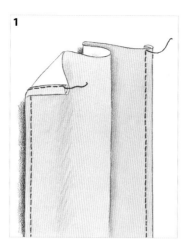

**1**

Pin the ruffle on the pillow so that the ruffle stitching line is on top of the chalk line. Determine how long the ruffle should be and sew the ruffle ends together using a French seam. Place this seam on the back side of the pillow.

Stitch the ruffle to the pillow along the ruffle stitching line. **3**

Starting at the center back, sew the decorative cording over the previous stitching of the ruffle. Use a cording foot to couch over the cording. **4**

To connect the ends of the cording on the back of the pillow, cut the ends so they butt together. Hand sew the ends together to hold in place. Fold a small piece of pillow fabric around the connection and hand tack in place.

Insert the pillow form.

**A contrasting wide satin ribbon can be substituted for a matching fabric ruffle.**

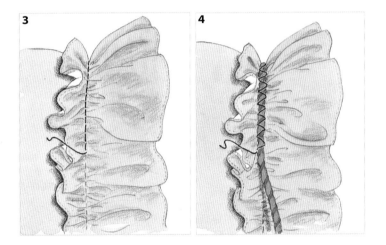

# pleats

# baby single
# **pleats**

**Finished size**

12" x 16"/30.5cm x 40.5cm

**Materials**

Fabric for pillow

Coordinating fabric for the ruffle

Pattern paper

Thread

12" x 16"/30.5cm x 40.5cm down
  pillow form

A narrow knife-pleated ruffle pillow can take on many looks depending on the fabrics you choose. For a formal look, use a stripe silk taffeta and a solid silk shantung, or go casual with a floral print cotton and a solid flannel.

**Preparation**

Cut 2 pieces of fabric 12" x 16"/30.5cm x 40.5cm for the pillow

Cut pieces of fabric 3"/7.6cm wide to make a strip 5yds/4.6m long

Draw parallel lines ¾"/1.9cm apart on strips of paper

**Calculate the amount of length for a pleated ruffle by multiplying the sum of the sides of the pillow times three.**

**To make the ruffle**

With right sides together, sew the strips of ruffle fabric together end to end to make one long strip. Press the seams open.

Fold the strip in half lengthwise with the wrong sides together. Baste ½"/1.3cm from the raw edges.

Place the strip on a piece of paper. Fold the fabric back on itself ¾"/1.9cm, lining up a fold with each pencil marking on the paper. Repeat to make continuous knife pleats. Pin or tape the pleats in place. Baste the pleats to the paper. **1**

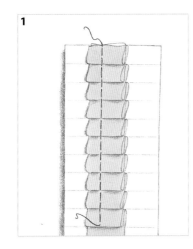

**1**

### To assemble the pillow

Starting in the middle of the bottom edge, pin the pleated ruffle to the right side of the pillow front. Determine where the ruffle ends meet. Remove the ruffle from the pillow and seam the ends together. Adjust the placement of the seam so that it is hidden within a pleat.

**When sewing the pillow together, work from the side of the previous stitching. Make sure the previous stitching is hidden in the seam allowance.**

Sew the ruffle to the right side of the pillow, easing the pleats through the corners. **2**

Sew the pillow front to the back, leaving an opening.

Turn the pillow to the right side. Insert the pillow form and slipstitch the opening closed.

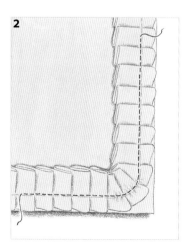

# box pleats
## and flat
## piping

**Finished size**

18" x 18"/45.5cm x 45.5cm

**Materials**

Fabric for the pillow

Fabric for the ruffle and piping

Pattern paper

Thread

18" x 18"/45.5cm x 45.5cm down
   pillow form

*Add a double dash of drama to a simple square pillow with narrow flat piping and a wide inverted pleated ruffle.
Use heavy silk damask for the pillow and silk taffeta for the trim.*

**Preparation**

Cut 2 pieces of fabric 19" x 19"/48.2cm x 48.2cm for the pillow

Cut strips of fabric 1½"/3.8cm wide to make 2¼yds/2m for the piping

Cut strips of fabric 5"/12.7cm wide to make 4 strips 60"/152.5cm long for the ruffle

Draw parallel lines 1½"/3.8cm apart on strips of paper

**To make the ruffle**

With right sides together, sew the ends of the ruffle strips. Press the seams open. Make four 60"/152.5cm
ruffle strips.

Instead of sewing mitered corners on the pleated ruffle, make more pleats in the same size and simply spread them around the corner. Be sure to ease the pleats at the corners to allow for the outside turns.

Fold each ruffle strip in half lengthwise with the wrong sides together and press. With right sides together, place the ends of two ruffle strips together. Starting at each seamline, draw a 45° angle extending towards the end. Stitch this line starting and stopping at the seam allowances. Trim the seam to ¼"/.6cm and across the corner. **1**

Turn the miter to the right side and lay the ruffle strip in a right angle on top of the paper. Match the seam allowance to a line on the paper. Fold the inverted pleats in place using the marked lines on the paper as guides. Baste pleats in place. Make six 3"/7.6cm pleats. **2**

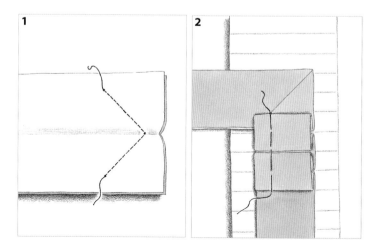

At the end of the sixth pleat, mark a dot on the seam allowance. With right sides together, pin another ruffle strip to the end of the pleated strip. Using the seam allowance dot as a starting point, draw a 45° angle and stitch. Trim the seam and point.

Turn the miter to the right side and repeat the pleating along the adjacent edge. Complete all four sides in the same manner. Hide the final seam in the miter.

**To assemble the pillow**
With right sides together, sew the ends of the piping strip to make one continuous piece. Press the seams open.

Fold the 1¹⁄₂"/3.8cm-wide piping strip in half lengthwise and press. With right sides together, pin the piping strip to the outside edges of the pillow front. Clip the seam allowance to turn the corners. To end the piping, open out the strip and sew a narrow seam. Press the seam open and fold in half again. **3**

With all raw edges together, pin the pleated ruffle over the piping to the pillow front and stitch all four sides.

Sew the pillow front to the back, leaving an opening.

Turn the pillow to the right side. Insert the pillow and slipstitch the opening closed.

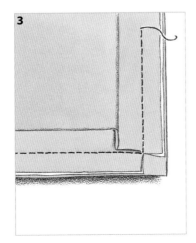

# corner **pleats**

**Finished size**
18" x 18"/45.5cm x 45.5cm

**Materials**
Fabric
Thread
18" x 18"/45.5cm x 45.5cm down
  pillow form

*Get creative when choosing your fabrics. This pillow is made in an extra-wide, four-color stripe silk faille. Three color stripes are used for the front and back, and the fourth color was used for the stately pleated ruffle. Add an ornate tasseled brocade trim for an extra-special designer touch.*

### Preparation

Cut 2 pieces of fabric 18" x 18"/45.5cm x 45.5cm
Cut strips of fabric 7"/17.8cm wide to make 4 strips 40"/101.5cm long for the ruffle
Draw 4 parallel lines on paper 1"/2.5cm apart

### To make the ruffle

With right sides together, sew the ends of the ruffle strips. Press the seams open. Make four 40"/101.5cm ruffle strips.

Fold each ruffle strip in half lengthwise with the wrong sides together and press. With right sides together, place the ends of two ruffle strips together. Starting at each seamline, draw a 45° angle extending towards the end. Stitch this line starting and stopping at the seam allowances. Trim the seam to ¼"/.6cm and across the point. **1**

Turn the miter to the right side and lay the ruffle strip in a right angle. Using the lined paper as a guide, fold three 1"/2.5cm knife pleats at the corner, aligning the first pleat at the seam allowance on the miter. **2**

**Press the trimmed miter seams open to eliminate extra bulk in the corners. Use a point turner to make the corners a perfect right angle.**

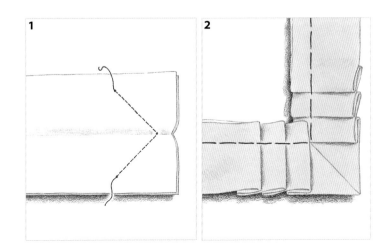

1

2

Fold three 1"/2.5cm knife pleats in the opposite direction at the other end of the strip, ending the last pleat at the seam allowance. Mark a dot at the seam allowance. With right sides together, pin another ruffle strip to the end of the pleated strip. Using the seam allowance dot as a starting point, draw a 45° angle and stitch. Trim the seam and point.

Turn the miter to the right side and repeat the pleating along the adjacent edge. Complete all four sides in the same manner. Hide the final seam in the miter.

**To assemble the pillow**

Matching the raw edges, pin the pleated ruffle to the pillow front and stitch all four sides. The unstitched portion of the miter seam allowances enables the ruffle to turn the corner without clipping.

Sew the pillow front to the back, leaving an opening.

Turn the pillow to the right side. Insert pillow and slipstitch the opening closed.

**If pins leave holes in your fabric or the fabric is too thick to pin effectively, keep the pleats in place temporarily using drafting tape.**

# flanges

all-in-one
# flange

**Finished size**
20" x 20"/51cm x 51cm

**Materials**
Fabric
Ribbon or decorative rayon thread
Thread
20" x 20"/51cm x 51cm down
  pillow form

*Go retro! A modern version of a 1940s cotton bark cloth, this over-sized pillow features a wide flange. For an authentic touch, conceal the flange's sewing line with narrow vintage ribbon, shown here, or with wide satin-stitching.*

### Preparation
Cut 1 piece of fabric 27" x 27"/68.5cm x 68.5cm for the pillow front
Cut 1 piece of fabric 15" x 27"/38cm x 68.5cm for the pillow back
Cut 1 piece of fabric 17$\frac{1}{2}$" x 27"/44.5cm x 68.5cm for the pillow back

### To assemble the pillow
Make an overlapping closure on the pillow back. See Basics page 13.

With right sides together, sew the front to the back around all four sides using a $\frac{1}{2}$"/1.3cm seam allowance. **1**

Turn to the right side and press the edges.

With tailor's chalk or a disappearing marker, draw a line 3"/7.6cm from the outside edges. Pin the front and back together along this line every few inches/centimeters. Stitch along the marked lines. **2**

**This flange design is ideal when the fabric has a large motif that is difficult to break up or the design is directional.**

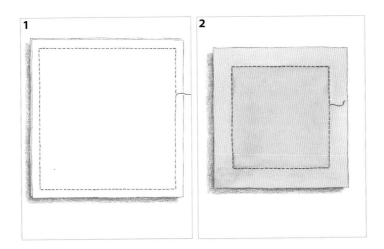

Using decorative rayon thread, sew a wide satin stitch over the previous stitching. **3**

### Option

Instead of the satin stitching, lay a narrow piece of ribbon over the straight stitching and stitch down the center.

Insert the pillow form through the back opening.

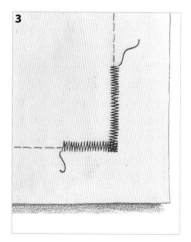

# contrasting
# mitered
# flange

**Finished size**
14" x 18"/35.5cm x 45.5cm

**Materials**
Fabric for pillow
Fabric for flange
Thread
14" x 18"/35.5cm x 45.5cm down
   pillow form

*A simple mitered flange can make a striking decorator statement when you partner a silk satin floral embroidered fabric with a bold contrasting silk taffeta.*

**Preparation**
Cut 1 piece of fabric 14" x 18"/35.5cm x 45.5cm for pillow front
Cut 1 piece of fabric 14" x 10½"/35.5cm x 26.5cm for pillow back
Cut 1 piece of fabric 14" x 13"/35.5cm x 33cm for pillow back
Cut strips of fabric 5"/12.7cm wide to make 72"/183cm for the flange

**To assemble the pillow**
Prepare the pillow back with an overlap closure. See Basics page 13.

With the wrong sides together, baste the pillow front and back together on the seamline around the outside edges.

**To make the flange**

Sew the 5"/12.7cm strips of fabric together end to end with the right sides together. Press the seams open.

With wrong sides together, press the flange in half lengthwise. Press each raw edge to the wrong side ½"/1.3cm.

With the right sides together, align one raw edge of the flange with one edge of the pillow. Sew along the seamline, starting and stopping ½"/1.3cm from the top and bottom edges of the pillow. Keep the opposite seam allowance folded in. **1**

Fold the flange diagonally away from the pillow at the seamline crossing point. Place a pin on the flange exactly 2"/1.3cm from the stitched seamline. **2**

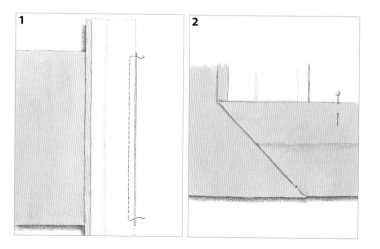

Fold the flange back on itself at the pin marking. Sew the flange to the adjacent edge of the pillow starting at the ending point of the previous stitching. **3**

Draw a line from the start of the previous stitching to a point where the center creaseline disappears into the outer fold and back to a point on the opposite edge of the flange that is perpendicular to the starting point. Sew on this line through the flange only. **4**

This is a good place to hide a seam in the flange. Instead of folding the flange back at the pin mark, sew a seam at the point where the pin marks the fold. **5**

Trim the excess flange. Press the seam allowances of the miter open and turn to the outside. The flange covers the seam allowance on both sides of the pillow. Slipstitch the flange to the back seam allowance. **6**

Insert the pillow form in the back opening.

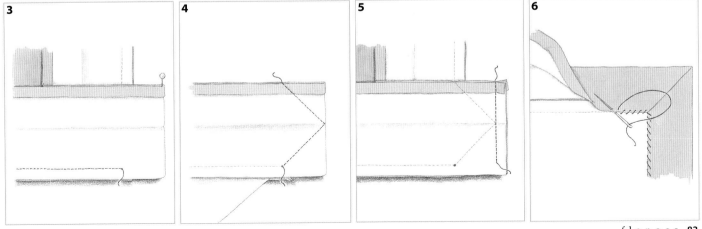

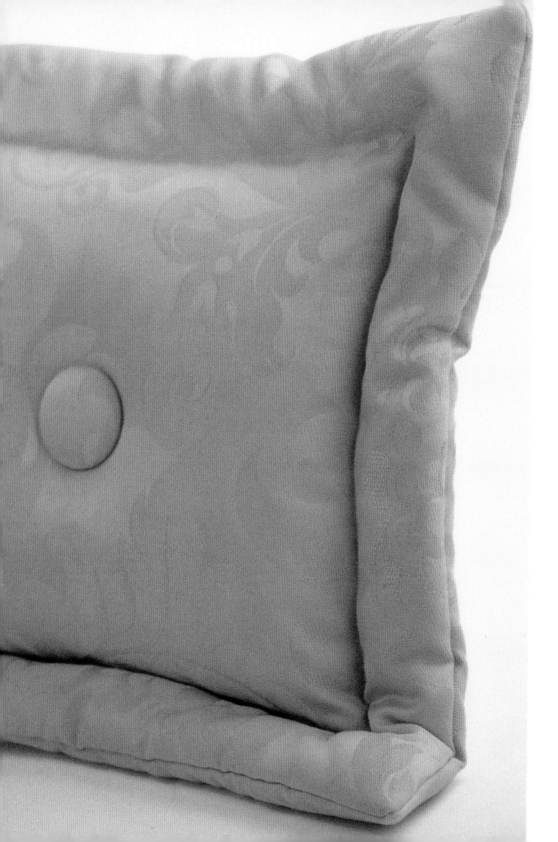

# padded **flang**

**Finished size**

12" x 22"/30.5cm x 56cm

**Materials**

Fabric

Wool batting

Cotton voile

4 large buttons to cover

Perle cotton

Fabric spray adhesive

Thread

12" x 22"/30.5cm x 56cm down
  pillow form

*Cozy up to this cushy over-sized pillow that's padded and stitched with a large seam allowance that creates a self flange. Embellish each side with a duo of extra-large, self-covered buttons.*

**Preparation**

Cut 1 piece of fabric 22" x 32"/56cm x 81.2cm for the pillow front
Cut 1 piece of fabric 17$\frac{1}{2}$" x 22"/44.5cm x 56cm for the pillow back
Cut 1 piece of fabric 20" x 22"/50.8cm x 56cm for the pillow back
Cut wool batting and cotton voile the same sizes as the pillow fabric
Cover 4 large buttons

**To assemble the pillow**

Layer the fabric, wool batting and cotton voile for each pillow section. Spray-glue the sections together before machine basting the outer edges. **1**

Prepare the pillow back with an overlap closure. See Basics page 13.

With right sides together, sew around the outside of the pillow using a 2$\frac{1}{2}$"/6.3cm seam allowance. **2**

Sewing through multiple layers of fabric and batting is easier when using a walking or even-feed presser foot.

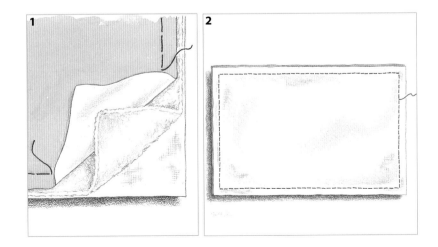

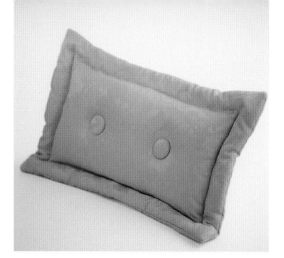

Trim across the corners, but do not trim the seam allowances. Turn the pillow to the right side. Topstitch 2¹/₂"/6.3cm from the outer edges. **3**

Insert the pillow form through the back opening.

Sew two sets of back-to-back buttons through the pillow. See Center Button project page 98.

3

# b a b y
# flange/
# pleated
# corners

**Finished size**

12" x 16"/30.5cm x 40.5cm

**Materials**

Fabric for pillow

Fabric for flange

Thread

12" x 16"/30.5cm x 40.5cm down
  pillow form

*Stitch up a smart lumbar pillow in a raw silk fabric and outline the edge with a narrow flange that has perky pleated corners.*

**Preparation**

Cut 2 pieces of fabric 12" x 16"/30.5cm x 40.5cm for the pillow

Cut strips of fabric 2"/5cm wide to make 70"/178cm for the flange

If the flange is cut on the bias, the corners will turn easier.

**To assemble the pillow**

With right sides together, sew the flange strips together end to end to make one long strip. Press the seams open.

With wrong sides together, fold the strip in half lengthwise. Do not press. Baste ¹/₂"/1.3cm from the fold.

Starting in the middle of one edge, pin the flange to the pillow front. Fold the flange back on itself ¹/₂"/1.3cm from one end and pin. **1**

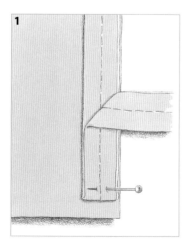

Fold a $^5/_8$"/1.6cm pleat. Clip the seam allowance at the corner. **2**

Turn the flange and fold another $^5/_8$"/1.6cm pleat. Continue the pleating at the remaining corners. Connect the ends of the flange neatly with a small seam within a pleat, if possible. Stitch the flange and pleats in place. **3**

With right sides together, sew the pillow front to the back, leaving an opening. Turn to the right side.

Insert the form and slipstitch the opening closed.

**A design variation is to run a gathering stitch along the flange seamline for about 3"/7.5cm. Draw up the gathering thread to create a soft, shirred corner.**

# scalloped
# **flange**

**Finished size**

22" x 22"/56cm x 56cm

**Materials**

Fabric

Cotton batting

Pattern paper

Tracing wheel and tracing paper

Thread

22" x 22"/56cm x 56cm down
  pillow form

*You can add fabulous texture and dimension to a cotton floral chintz pillow, when you machine-quilt the center motif using matching threads. The cotton batting backing also provides extra body to the wide scallop flange.*

## Preparation

Cut 1 piece of fabric 28" x 28"/71cm x 71cm for the pillow front
Cut 1 piece of fabric 15½" x 28"/39.5cm x 71cm for the pillow back
Cut 1 piece of fabric 18" x 28"/45.5cm x 71cm for the pillow back
Cut 1 piece of batting 28" x 28"/71cm x 71cm

## To make the scallop template

On a large piece of paper, draw a 22"/56cm long line. Draw perpendicular lines at each end for about 5"/12.5cm. Draw lines extending 2½"/6.5cm out from the previous lines. The outer long line is now 27"/68.5cm long. Draw another line ¾"/2cm inside and parallel to the outside line.

Mark the 27"/68.5cm outside line in half, in fourths and in eighths. Using the outside line as the peak and the next parallel line as the valley, draw five soft scallops. Round the corners to match the shape of the scallops.

## To assemble the pillow

Prepare the pillow back with an overlap closure. See Basics page 13.

Layer the cotton batting under the pillow front. Pin frequently and outline quilt the central motif.

Lay the paper template along one edge of the wrong side of the pillow front, placing the peak of the scallops on the ½"/1.5cm seam allowance. Using tracing wheel and tracing paper, mark the outer scallop line. Move the template to repeat the markings on the remaining three edges.

**Once you get one scallop drawn to your liking, make a paper or tag board template of the shape and use it as a drawing guide for the remaining scallops.**

With right sides together, sew the pillow front to the back along the marked scallop lines. Use a walking or even-feed presser foot to prevent creeping. **1**

Trim the seams to $^1/_8$"/.3cm and turn the pillow to the right side. Press the edges.

With the wrong sides together, stitch the front to the back $2^1/_2$"/6.5cm from the peak of the scallops. **2**

Insert the pillow form through the back opening.

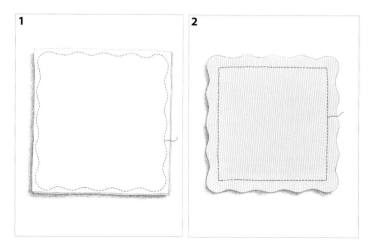

# double
# flange

**Finished size**

14" x 14"/35.5cm x 35.5cm

**Materials**

Fabric

Tagboard or manila file folder

Thread

14" x 14"/35.5cm x 35.5cm down
  pillow form

*A crisp linen fabric patterned with a subtle, yet graphic rope 'n tassel design makes the perfect choice for the tai-
lored style of this double flange pillow. The flange is formed by stitching a double layer of mitered hems together.*

**Preparation**

Cut 2 pieces of fabric 23" x 23"/58.5cm x 58.5cm

Cut 1 tagboard strip 2½"/6.3cm wide by 12"/30.5cm long

**To miter the corners**

On the wrong side of one pillow piece, place the tagboard template about 2½"/6.3cm from a raw edge. Press
the fabric up and over the template, matching the raw edge to the top of the template. Move the template to
press the entire edge. Repeat this process to press 2½"/6.3cm to the wrong side of all edges of the pillow front
and back.

When stitching the fourth and final side, try using a zipper foot. Having the pillow form inside the pillow makes it difficult to sew straight, so go slowly and adjust your presser foot position often.

At one corner, press the hems in place again. On adjacent sides of a corner where the two hems intersect, place pins through the hem only. **1**

Unfold the hem. With right sides together, align the raw edges, matching the pins. Draw a line from the pins to a point on the diagonal fold where the creaseline intersects. Stitch this line. **2**

Trim the excess fabric at the corner to $1/4$"/.6cm. Press the seam open over a point presser and turn the corner to the outside, forming the miter.

Repeat for all corners on the front and back of the pillow.

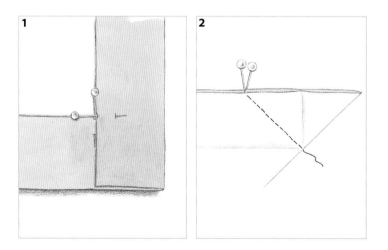

**To assemble the pillow**

With wrong sides together, stitch the front to the back 2"/5cm from the edge of three sides. Insert the pillow form.

Place pins along the fourth seamline to anchor well and prevent slipping. Stitch the fourth side.

# buttons

# center **button**

**Finished size**

12"/30.5cm-diameter x 6"/15cm-deep

**Materials**

Fabric for pillow

Contrasting fabric for piping

Cotton cable cord

Compass

2 large buttons with shanks

Perle cotton cord

Upholstery needle

Thread

12" x 6"/30.5cm x 15cm down
  pillow form

*Silk plaid piping adds a kaleidoscope of color to this plump round box pillow. Other pro details include back-to-back buttons attached through the pillow form, that fasten through the buttonholes of the pillow cover making the cover easy to remove.*

### Preparation

Cut 2 pieces of fabric 12"/30.5cm diameter for front and back
Cut 1 piece of fabric 6" x 39¹/₂"/15cm x 100.5cm long for the boxing
Cut 2 pieces of cable cord 39¹/₂"/100.5cm
Cut pieces of bias fabric 2"/5cm wide to make 2 lengths 39¹/₂"/100.5cm

### To assemble the pillow

Make one buttonhole in the center of each fabric circle.

Make two lengths of covering piping. See Basics page 10.

Sew the covered piping to the outside edge of each circle, clipping the flange often. **1**
See Basics page 11.

Staystitch the long edges of the pillow boxing and clip often.

With right sides together, sew the short ends of the boxing together. Press the seam open.

With right sides together, sew one clipped edge of the boxing to the outer edge of one pillow front. **2**

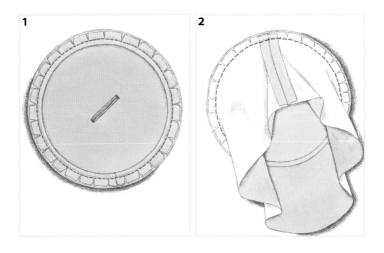

Sew the other clipped edge of the boxing to the pillow back, leaving an opening.

**A compass is the obvious circle-making tool, but plates, trays, wastebaskets and other common household items make great templates for drawing circles.**

Attach the buttons to the center of the pillow form. To begin, tie about a 15"/38cm length of perle cotton cord securely to the shank of one button. Thread the opposite end of the cord through an upholstery needle. Thread the needle through the center of the pillow form, then through the shank of the second button. Pull the cord tight and tie off onto the button shank. **3**

Insert the pillow form and slipstitch the opening closed.

Slip the buttons on the pillow form through the center buttonholes.

**3**

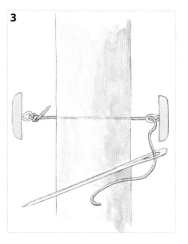

# button
# overlap

**Finished size**

20" x 26"/51cm x 66cm

**Materials**

Fabric for pillow

Fabric for band

4 buttons

Thread

20" x 26"/51cm x 66cm down
   pillow form

*Accent your bedroom décor with a pretty pillow sham made in a washed cotton floral print. It features a wide contrasting color button band that fastens closed with four big pearl buttons.*

**Preparation**

Cut 1 piece of fabric 20" x 26"/51cm x 66cm for pillow back

Cut 1 piece of fabric 12¹/₂" x 26"/31.7cm x 66cm for top front

Cut 1 piece of fabric 11¹/₂" x 26"/29.2cm x 66cm for bottom front

Cut 1 piece of fabric 7" x 26"/17.7cm x 66cm for band

**To assemble the pillow**

Serge-finish one long edge of the band. Press in half lengthwise with the wrong sides together. **1**

With right sides together, sew the unfinished edge of the band to the bottom edge of the top front. Press seam toward the band. **2**

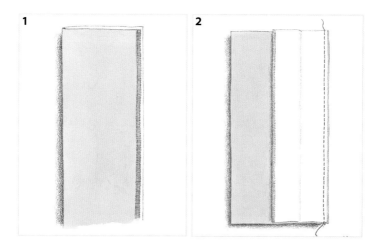

Fold the band along the creaseline and stitch in the ditch to attach the band. Make four buttonholes evenly spaced on the band. **3**

Serge-finish the top edge of the bottom front. Fold 3$\frac{1}{2}$"/8.9cm of the top edge to the wrong side. Topstitch 3"/7.6cm from the edge. Baste the top front over the bottom front to make a piece of fabric that is 20"/51cm high.

With right sides together, sew the front to the back around all sides. Turn to the right side.

Sew buttons to the bottom front corresponding to the buttonholes.

Insert the pillow form.

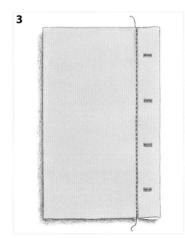

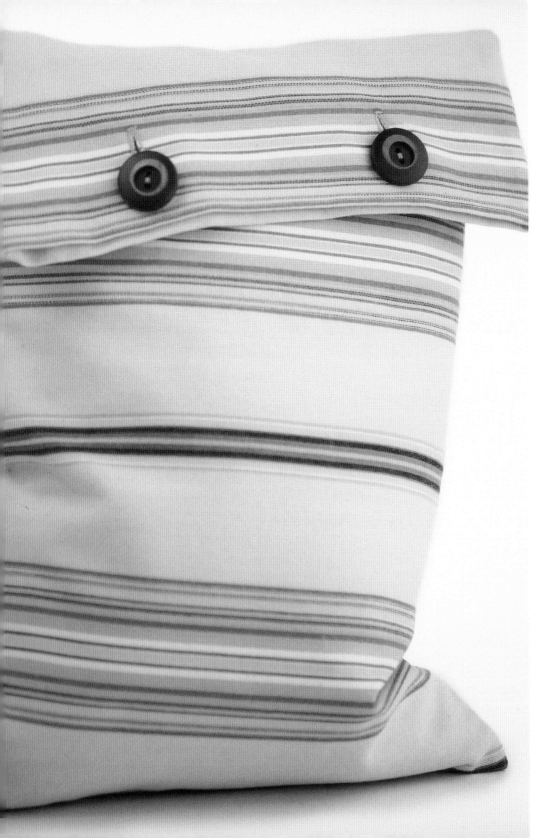

# cufflink
# **buttons**

**Finished size**

12" x 16"/30.5cm x 40.5cm

**Materials**

Fabric

4 two-hole buttons

Thread

12" x 16"/30.5cm x 40.5cm down
  pillow form

*Just about anything goes when it comes to choosing fabrics. Here, a striped tablecloth was used to make a tailored pillowcase that's accented with novel "cufflink" buttons that fasten through buttonholes on both sides.*

### Preparation
Cut 2 pieces of fabric 13" x 22½"/33cm x 57cm

### To assemble the pillow
With right sides together, sew the pillow front to the back around three sides, leaving one short end open.

To make a finished hem on the open end, press ½"/1.3cm to the wrong side. Press an additional 2½"/6.3cm to the wrong side and topstitch the hem in place. **1**

Make two machine buttonholes on the front hem and two buttonholes on the back hem, placing them exactly opposite one another.

### To make the cufflink buttons
Thread a sewing needle with double thread. Knot the end of the thread. Insert the needle through one hole in the button from the back side. Insert the needle back through the button and between the two threads right above the knot to secure the thread on the back of the button.

Join the two buttons together with a ½"/1.3cm shank of several passes of the thread. Wrap the thread around the shank several times, pass it once again through one button and slide the needle under the wraps before knotting the thread or securing it with a few stitches, then cut the excess thread. **2**

**The length of the shank is determined by the thickness of the fabric. The heavier the fabric, the longer the shank.**

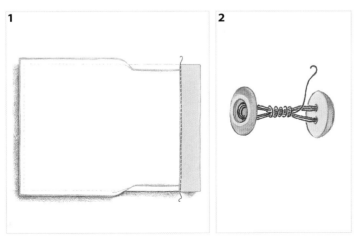

1

2

# button **toggle**

**Finished size**

7" x 11"/17.5cm x 28cm

**Materials**

Fabric

Fabric for lining

Embroidery floss

Tassel

2 buttons

Buttonhole twist thread

Thread

Muslin

Polyester filling

*Think outside the box when it comes to pillow shapes. This novel triangular pillow is made in a striped damask upholstery fabric and completely lined in a solid silk dupioni. The end triangles are hand-sewn using a decorative blanket stitch. Fashion your own toggle closure with a pair of vintage rhinestone buttons and a glitzy metallic tassel.*

### Preparation

Cut 1 piece of fabric 12" x 25"/30.5cm x 63.5cm for the pillow body
Cut 2 triangles of fabric 7" x 6" x 7"/17.8cm x 15.2cm x 17.8cm for the pillow ends
Cut 1 piece of lining 12" x 25"/30.5cm x 63.5cm for the pillow body
Cut 2 triangles of lining 7" x 6" x 7"/17.8cm x 15.2cm x 17.8cm for the pillow ends
Cut 1 piece of muslin 12" x 21"/30.5cm x 53.3cm for the pillow form
Cut 2 triangles of muslin 7" x 6" x 7"/17.8cm x 15.2cm x 17.8cm for the pillow form ends

### To assemble the pillow

With right sides together, sew the fabric body and the two end triangles to the corresponding lining pieces, leaving openings in each piece. Sew the corners slightly rounded. Trim the seam allowances and turn each section to the right side. Slipstitch the openings closed. **1**

With the wrong sides together, pin the bottom of one triangle 6"/15.2cm from one end of the pillow body along one long edge. **2**

Bring the end of the pillow body to the top of the triangle and pin. Starting at the top of the triangle and working down one edge, hand-sew the two finished edges together using three strands of embroidery floss and a blanket stitch. Stitch all three sides of the triangle. **3**

Repeat for the other triangle. **4**

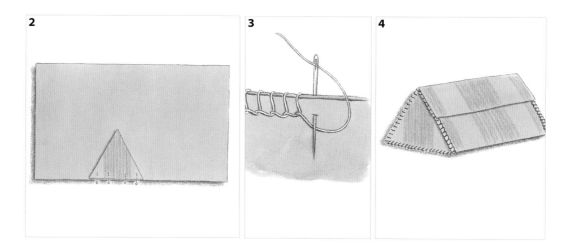

**The tassel used on this project originally had two tassels, one at each end of a length of cord. This type of tassel is typically used as a chair tie to attach cushions to arms or legs with a decorative flair.**

Sew one button on the flap and another button on the pillow.

If the tassel has a loop cord or two tails, cut one cord at the head of the tassel. Wrap the single cord around the two buttons to measure the length needed for the toggle.

At the appropriate length, lay buttonhole twist on top of the tassel cords, leaving a loop. **5**

Wrap the twist around the cords several times until the cords are held together securely. Thread the end of the twist through the loop and pull the starting end until the loop and twist end are hidden under the wrapping. **6**

Cut the excess twist and the excess tassel cord. **7**

Make a muslin shell in the shape of the pillow and stuff it with polyester filling. Insert the pillow form into the pillow. Wrap the tassel toggle around the two buttons.

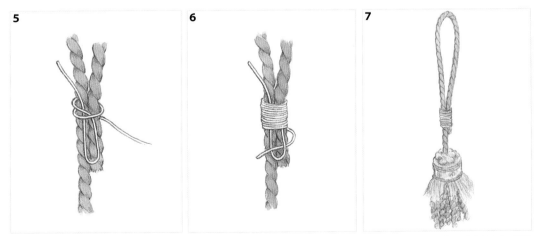

# button **hankie**

**Finished size**

16" x 16"/40.5cm x 40.5cm

**Materials**

Fabric for pillow

Fabric for hankie

Braid trim

4 buttons

Thread

16" x 16"/40.5cm x 40.5cm down

 pillow form

*Showcase a whimsical machine-embroidered hankie on a background of denim blue. Sew the mitered corner square from sheer handkerchief linen. Topstitch in place, then dot each corner with pearly white buttons.*

**Preparation**

Cut 2 pieces of fabric 16" x 16"/40.5cm x 40.5cm for the pillow

Cut 1 piece of fabric 10½" x 10½"/26.5cm x 26.5cm for the hankie

Cut 1 piece of braid trim 66"/167.5cm long

**To make the hankie**

Machine-embroider the Art Stars design in the center of the hankie. See Resources page 143 for information on how to obtain the Art Stars embroidery design.

Press the four sides of the hankie 1½"/4cm to the wrong side. **1**

With hems pressed in place, insert pins in the hem only exactly where the two hems intersect. **2**

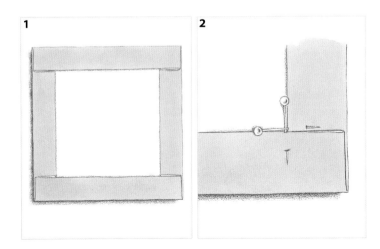

Open out the hems and position them with the right sides together, matching the pins at the raw edges. Stitch from the pins to the hem creaseline at the diagonal fold. **3**

Trim the seam to $1/4$"/.5cm. **4**

Press the seams open over a point presser and turn the hems to the wrong side.

Pin the mitered hankie in the center of the pillow front. Stitch $1^1/_8$"/2.8cm from the finished edges on all sides. **5**

Sew a button in each corner of the mitered hankie.

**Vintage linens such as hankies, napkins, tea towels and tablecloths found in flea markets and antique shops provide ample inspiration for embroidered fragments.**

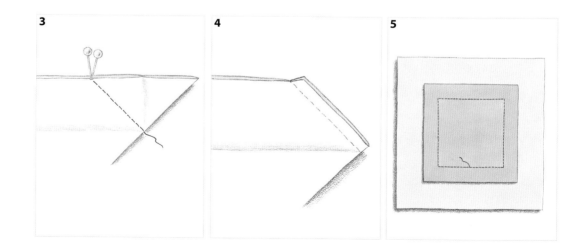

**To assemble the pillow**

Sew the braid trim to the outer edges of the pillow front. See Basics pages 11-12.

With right sides together, sew the pillow front to the back, leaving an opening.

Insert the form and slipstitch the opening closed.

ties

# end **ties**

**Finished size**
20" x 26"/51cm x 66cm

**Materials**
Fabric
Bodkin
Thread
20" x 26"/51cm x 66cm down
 pillow form

*The soft and relaxed look of this faded floral print pillow sham is achieved by cutting the pillow larger than the form and loosely tying the ends together. An inside flap conceals the pillow form from view.*

### Preparation
Cut 1 piece of fabric 21" x 27"/53.3cm x 68.5cm for pillow top
Cut 1 piece of fabric 21½" x 27"/54.6cm x 68.5cm for pillow bottom
Cut 1 piece of fabric 7½" x 27"/19cm x 68.5cm for the inside flap
Cut 6 pieces of fabric cut on the bias 1½"/3.8cm wide by 12"/30.5cm long

### To make ties
Fold each strip of bias in half lengthwise with the right sides together. Stitch ½"/1.3cm from the folded edge. Trim the seam to ¼"/.5cm.

Insert a bodkin down the center of the tube and sew the eye of the bodkin to the top of one tube. Feed the bodkin through the tube, turning the bias strip to the right side. Make six ties.

### To assemble the pillow
On the right side of the pillow front, pin the ends of three ties even with the raw edge, evenly spaced.

Turn one long edge of the flap to the wrong side 1"/2.5cm and press. Fold the raw edge to the creaseline and press a double ½"/1.3cm seam. Topstitch.

With the right sides together, stitch the raw edge of the flap to one long edge of the pillow front, sandwiching the ties. Finish the raw edges together. **1**

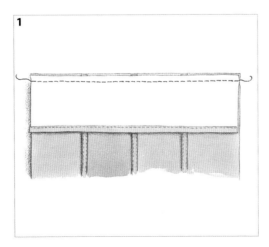

1

Turn one long edge of the pillow back to the wrong side 1"/2.5cm and press. Fold the raw edge to the creaseline and press a double ½"/1.3cm seam. Insert the remaining three ties under the hem evenly spaced to match the other tie placements. Topstitch the hem, catching the ties at the same time.

**When the ties are cut on the bias, the ends will not ravel, so there is no need to hem or finish them other than the knots.**

Open out the flap and with right sides together, place the hemmed edge of the back at the well of the seam, sandwiching the back between the front and the flap. Leaving the flap edge alone, stitch three sides of the pillow. Turn to the outside. **2**

Trim ties evenly and knot the ends.

Insert the pillow form, placing the form under the flap.

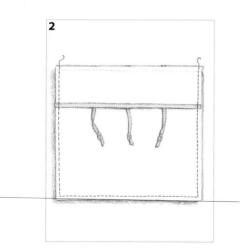

# top **ties**

**Finished size**
18" x 18"/45.5cm x 45.5cm

**Materials**
Fabric
Compass
Drawing paper
Thread
18" x 18"/45.5cm x 45.5cm down
  pillow form

*Go graphic with a curvy scallop flange pillow stitched up in a bold striped linen fabric. Three ties fasten the pillow
closed and add an interesting touch.*

**Preparation**
Make a paper template of a scallop design using a compass.

Cut 1 piece of fabric 22$\frac{1}{2}$" x 22$\frac{1}{2}$"/57cm x 57cm for the back
Cut 2 piece of fabric 12$\frac{1}{4}$" x 22$\frac{1}{2}$"/28.5cm x 57cm for the overlap
Cut 1 piece of fabric 15$\frac{1}{4}$" x 22$\frac{1}{2}$"/38.7cm x 57cm for the underlap
Cut 6 strips of fabric 1$\frac{1}{2}$" x 12"/3.8cm x 30.5cm for the ties

**To make the ties**
Fold each strip in half lengthwise and press. Open out the strip and fold each raw edge to the center creaseline
and press. Edgestitch each edge.

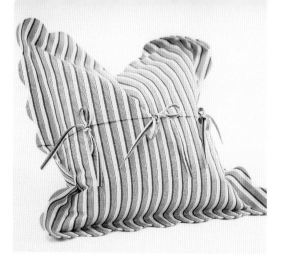

It is easier to make one long strip first and then cut it into 6"/15.2cm sections.

**To assemble the pillow**

Press the bottom edge of the overlap to the wrong side 1"/2.5cm. Fold the raw edge to the creaseline and press a double ½"/1.3cm hem.

Insert one end of three ties into the hem, placing one in the center and evenly spacing the other two ties. Topstitch the hem catching the tie in the hem. **1**

Make a ½"/1.3cm double hem at the top edge of the underlap.

Mark a horizontal line 3"/7.6cm below the top edge of the underlap. Place the overlap along the center line marking.

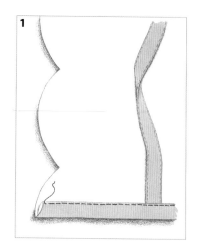

Position the ties on the underlap about ³/₄"/1.9cm from the overlap edge and in line with the overlap ties. Stitch about ¹/₄"/.6cm from the raw edge of the tie. **2**

Trim the end of the tie to about ¹/₈"/.3cm. Fold the tie back over itself to cover the raw edge and stitch.

Position the overlap over the underlap and baste the side edges.

**Start the stitching along a side rather than at a corner so the corners are secure.**

With right sides together, stitch the outer scalloped edge using a ¹/₄"/.6cm seam and pivoting at each scallop connection point. Trim seam to ¹/₈"/.3cm. Clip to each pivot point. Turn the pillow to the outside and press.

With wrong sides together, stitch a line around all sides of the pillow 2"/5cm from the outer edge of the scallops.

Insert the pillow form. Tie the ties in a bow and knot each end.

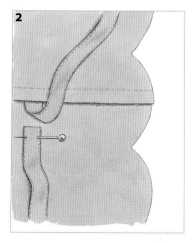

# side **ties**

**Finished size**

20"/51cm square x 2½"/6.3cm deep.

**Materials**

Fabric for center accents

Fabric for corners, boxing, cording
 and ties

Moss fringe

Cotton cable cord

Cotton batting (optional)

Pattern paper

Thread

20" x 20" x 2½"/51cm x 51cm x 6.3cm
 down pillow form

*This generously-sized box pillow is made in a combination of cotton toile and a wide tone-on-tone stripe. The central motif, set on the diagonal, is outlined in a thick cotton moss fringe. Matching ties, nestled in the side seams, pinch the shape and create added interest.*

### Preparation

Draw a 19"/48.2cm square on a piece of paper. Mark the center of each edge. Draw a square on the diagonal, connecting the dots on each edge.

Cut out the square and add seam allowances

Cut out one triangle and add seam allowances

Cut 2 pieces of accent fabric using the paper template

Cut 8 triangles using the paper template

Cut strips of fabric 3½"/8.9cm wide to make 85"/216cm-long for boxing

Cut 4 strips of fabric on the bias 2" x 12"/5cm x 30.5cm for the ties

Cut 2 pieces off cotton batting using the paper template for the accents

Cut a strip of moss fringe 65"/165cm

Cut strips of fabric on the bias 2"/5cm wide to make cording 5yds/4.6m long

### To make the ties

Make four ties. See End Ties page 116.

### To assemble the pillow

Baste the cotton flannel to the wrong side of the center accent pieces (optional).

Sew the moss fringe to the right side of the outside edge of the front center accent piece. See Basics pages 10-11.

With right sides together, sew the long side of a triangle to one edge of the center accent piece. Stop the stitching ½"/1.3cm from each end. Repeat for the remaining three triangles for both the front and back. **1**

With right sides together, sew the diagonal edges of the triangles to complete the pillow front and back. Press the seams open.

Pin one tie to each point where the accent piece ends at each side on the front and the back. **2**

Make enough covered cording to edge the front and the back. See Basics page 10.

Sew covered cording to the right sides of both the front and the back, sewing over the ties at each side. See Basics pages 10-11.

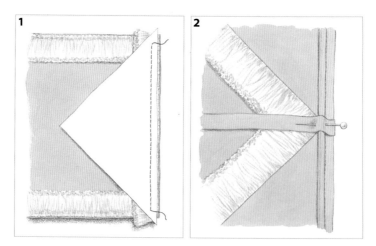

Most moss fringes come with the fluffy ends sewn together with a heavy thread. Leave the stitching in the fringe while sewing it to the pillow and remove it when the pillow is completed. Then fluff the fringe with a pick-like comb.

Sew strips of the band together to make a continuous 80"/203.2cm strip. Starting in the center of the right side of one edge of the front, sew the band to the outer edges, clipping at the corners. See Basics pages 9-10. Sew a seam to connect the ends of the band. Press the seam open.

Sew the other raw edge of the band to the right side of the pillow back, leaving an opening along one edge.

Insert the pillow form and slipstitch the opening closed.

Tie the ties, cinching in the side boxing.

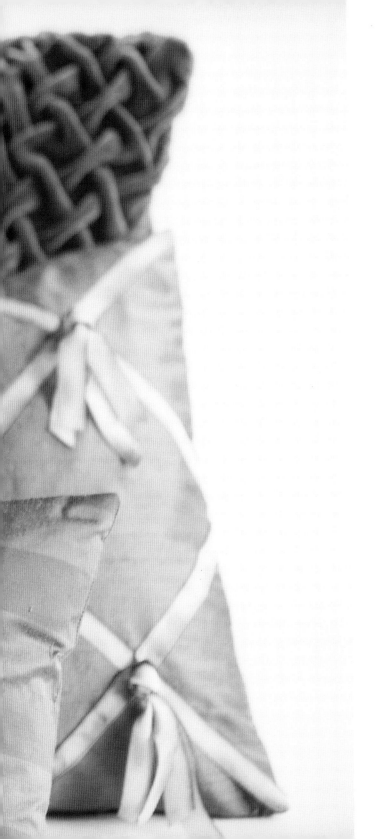

# embellishments

# trellis **ribbon**

**Finished size**
14" x 14"/35.5cm x 35.5cm

**Materials**
Fabric
Ribbon
Fine Fusing Tape
Thread
14" x 14"/35.5cm x 35.5cm down
  pillow form

*Silk dupioni makes the perfect background for a trellis pattern of bias-cut, hand-dyed silk ribbons. Knotted ribbon ends create interesting texture and dimension.*

### Preparation
Cut 2 pieces of fabric 14" x 14"/35.5cm x 35.5cm
Cut 5yds/4.6m of ribbon

> **Lightweight fabrics such as silk dupioni need to be stabilized with a fusible interfacing.**

### To embellish the pillow
On the pillow front, mark an X from corner to corner and parallel lines to the X that intersect the center of each edge.

Fuse strips of Fine Fusing Tape over the marked lines. Remove the paper to expose the line of glue. **1**

Fuse strips of ribbon to each section. Where the ribbons cross, stop each section of ribbon and leave a 6"/15.2cm tail. Edgestitch both edges of the ribbon, stopping at the intersections and backstitching. **2**

### To assemble the pillow
With right sides together, sew the pillow front to the back, leaving an opening along one edge.

Insert the pillow form. Slipstitch the opening closed.

Tie the ends of the ribbons at each intersection. Trim the ends on the diagonal. **3**

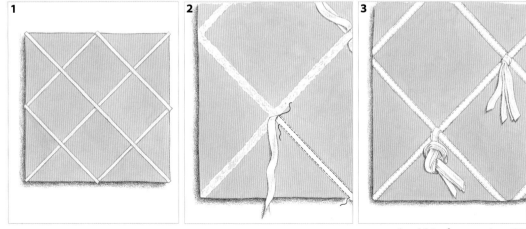

# pieced

**Finished size**

12" x 16"/30.5cm x 40.5cm

**Materials**

Fabric

4 accent fabrics

Thread

12" x 16"/30.5cm x 40.5cm down
 pillow form

*Use a sensational selection of vintage kimono fabrics along with a pretty tone-on-tone silk stripe to fashion this beautiful lumbar size pillow.*

### Preparation

Cut 2 pieces of fabric 8¹⁄₂" x 12"/21.5cm x 30.5cm

Cut 2 pieces of fabric 2¹⁄₂" x 12"/6.3cm x 30.5cm

Cut 2 pieces of one accent fabric 3¹⁄₂" x 12"/8.9cm x 30.5cm

Cut 2 pieces of one accent fabric 3¹⁄₂" x 12"/8.9cm x 30.5cm

Cut 2 pieces of one accent fabric 3¹⁄₂" x 2¹⁄₂"/8.9cm x 6.3cm

Stabilize lightweight fabrics if needed

### To assemble the pillow

Press ¹⁄₂"/1.3cm to the wrong side of the top and bottom of the small accent patches. **1**

Place one small accent patch 3¹⁄₂"/8.9cm from the top of one long accent strip. Edgestitch both folded edges. **2**

To assemble the pillow front, sew the narrow strip of fabric to the left edge of the pieced strip with the right sides together. Press the seam open. **3**

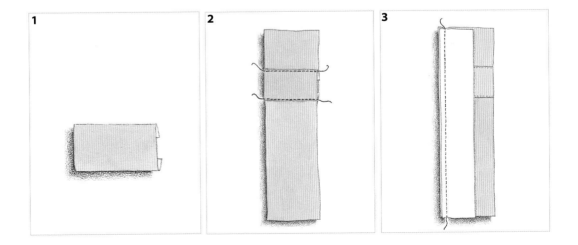

**To achieve perfect seam alignment when joining the front and the back, fuse a strip of Fine Fusing Tape on the seam allowance and then "glue" the seams together before sewing.**

With right sides together, sew one accent strip to the right edge of the pieced strip. Press the seam open. **4**

With right sides together, sew the remaining fabric piece to the right edge of the accent strip. Press seam open. **5**

To assemble the pillow back, reverse the piecing order so that the seamlines will align at the top and bottom edges.

With right sides together, sew the pillow front to the back, leaving an opening.

Insert the pillow form and slipstitch the opening closed.

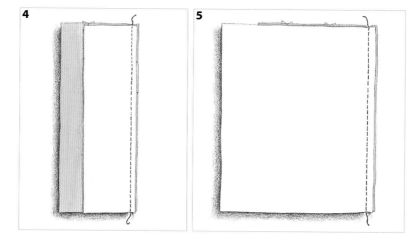

# w r a p

## Finished size

12" x 16"/30.5cm x 40.5cm

## Materials

Fabric

Accent fabric

Cotton flannel

Twisted cord

Button

Thread

12" x 16"/30.5cm x 40.5cm down
   pillow form

*Wrap and tie a tone-on-tone stripe silk taffeta pillow with a novel obi-style sash, then embellish with a vintage bakelite button.*

### Preparation

Cut 2 pieces of fabric 12" x 16"/30.5cm x 40.5cm

Cut 2 pieces of accent fabric 6½" x 26"/16.5cm x 66cm

Cut 1 piece of cotton flannel 6½" x 26"/16.5cm x 66cm

Cut 2 pieces of twisted cord 30"/76.5cm long

### To assemble the pillow

With right sides together, sew the pillow front to the back, leaving an opening. Insert the pillow form and slipstitch the opening.

### To make the obi

Baste one layer of cotton flannel to the wrong side of one accent fabric.

With right sides together, sew the two accent pieces together, leaving an opening. Press the seams open first, then turn the fabric to the right side and press lightly. Slipstitch the opening closed. **1**

**1**

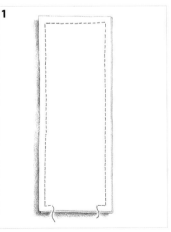

**To eliminate puckers when sewing crisp fabric such as silk taffeta, press the seam flat (meld) first before pressing a seam open or turning an edge.**

Wrap the accent fabric around the pillow, overlapping one end over the slipstitched end. Pin in place.

Pair two lengths of twisted cord. Tie a knot in the center of the cord length. Thread the ends of the cord through the holes in the button, allowing the knot to sit on top. Wrap the cords around the pillow.

On the back of the pillow, align the cords and wrap a few strands of thread around the cords to secure. Cut the excess cording. **2**

Fold a small scrap of accent fabric with the raw edges to the center and encase the thread wrapping on the cord. Fold the raw edges under and slipstitch. **3**

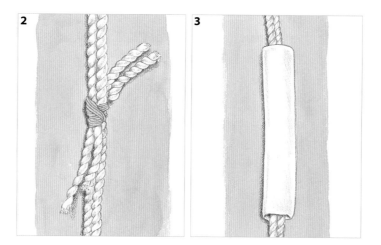

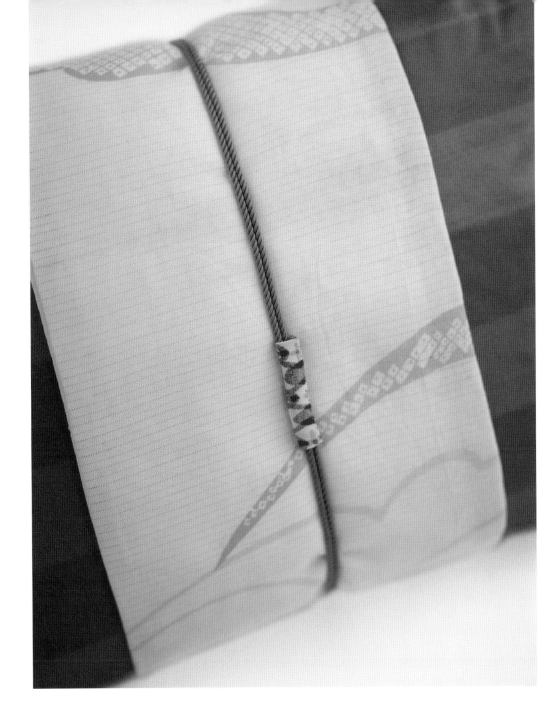

# tassel fringe

**Finished size**

12" x 12"/30.5cm x 30.5cm

**Materials**

Fabric

Tassel fringe

Eyelash trim

Fine Fusing Tape

Thread

12" x 12"/30.5cm x 30.5cm down
 pillow form

*The ultra-rich textures of silk brocade fabric, petite tassel fringe and wispy eyelash trim make the most sumptuous of pillows. To get the same look, be sure to match colors perfectly.*

### Preparation

Cut 2 pieces of fabric 12" x 12"/30.5cm x 30.5cm

Cut 10 pieces of tassel fringe 12"/30.5cm each

Cut 1 piece of eyelash trim 50"/127cm long

### To assemble the pillow

Starting 2"/5cm from the bottom of the pillow front, draw five parallel chalk lines ³/₄"/1.9cm apart.

Fuse the Fine Fusing Tape to the back of the tassel fringe flange. Remove the paper.

Starting at the bottom, fuse one strip of tassel fringe to the right side of the pillow. Stitch along the top of the flange. **1**

Fuse the second row of fringe and stitch. Repeat for the next three rows.

Sew five rows of fringe to the pillow back in the same manner as the front.

Trim the tassels out of the seam allowances and pin other tassels out of the way.

With right sides together, use ¹/₂"/1.3cm seam allowance to sew the pillow front to the back, leaving an opening. Turn the pillow to the right side.

Insert the pillow form and slipstitch the opening closed.

Hand-sew the eyelash trim to the well of the seam on all four sides, overlapping the trim to end.

**The placement of the first row of trim and the distance between rows are determined by the length of the tassels on the trim. Adjust as necessary.**

# s a s h i k o

**Finished size**
16" x 16"/40.5cm x 40.5cm

**Materials**
Fabric
Accent fabric
Cotton batting
Embroidery floss
Tiger Tape™
Thread
16" x 16"/40.5cm x 40.5cm down
 pillow form

*Combine three boldly contrasting colored silk fabrics in a stunning asymmetrical arrangement to create a pillow packed with visual appeal. Add an exotic touch with sashiko embroidery, a simple technique of carefully sewn running stitches done in cotton floss.*

**Preparation**

Cut 2 pieces of fabric 11¹/₂" x 16"/29.2cm x 40.5cm

Cut 2 pieces of fabric 6" x 16"/15.2cm x 40.5cm

Cut 2 pieces of accent fabric 2" x 16"/10cm x 40.5cm

Cut 2 pieces cotton batting 16" x 16"/40.5cm x 40.5cm

**To assemble the pillow**

Fold an accent strip of fabric in half lengthwise with the wrong sides together. Baste ¹/₂"/1.3cm from the fold.

With right sides together, sew the accent strip to one long edge of the 6"/15.2cm wide piece of fabric. **1**

With right sides together, sew the 11¹/₂"/29.2cm piece of fabric to the narrower piece, sandwiching the accent trim. Press the seam towards the larger piece. **2**

Pin one layer of cotton batting to the wrong side of the pillow front and baste around all edges.

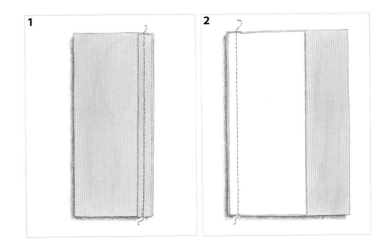

**To sashiko stitch**

Mark parallel lines 2"/5cm apart on the larger section of the pillow front.

Using six strands of embroidery floss and working from the top side, hand sew a running stitch on each marked line. **3**

Repeat the above steps for the pillow back, but reverse the piecing so that the seams line up from the front to the back.

With right sides together, sew the pillow front to the back, leaving an opening.

Insert the pillow and slipstitch the opening closed.

Lay a strip of Tiger Tape™ marked in ¹⁄₄"/.6cm increments next to each sewing line on the pillow. This will help you evenly space your stitching.

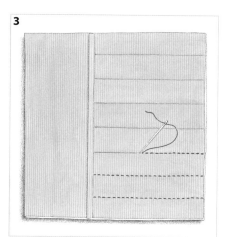

3

# reversed
## smocked

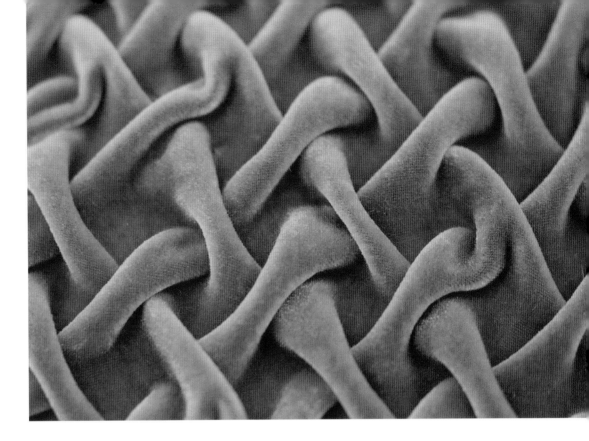

**Finished size**

16" x 16"/40.5cm x 40.5cm

**Materials**

Fabric

Polyester thread

Muslin

16" x 16"/40.5cm x 40.5cm down
 pillow form

*This elegant pillow is made in a luxurious silk and rayon iridescent velvet. The dazzling smocked lattice pattern that graces the front is done by hand on the reverse side of the fabric.*

**Preparation**

Cut 1 piece of fabric 32" x 32"/81.2cm x 81.2cm for the front

Cut 1 piece of fabric 16" x 16"/40.5cm x 40.5cm for the back

Cut 1 piece of muslin 16" x 16"/40.5cm x 40.5cm

**To reverse smock**

Using the design grid as a guide, mark the grid on the wrong side of the fabric using a pencil or a non-bleeding marking pen.

Thread a sewing needle with polyester thread slightly longer than the width of the fabric. Knot one end. Pick up a small amount of fabric at A, then pick up dot B, then dot A again, pulling A and B tightly together with a small stitch. **1**

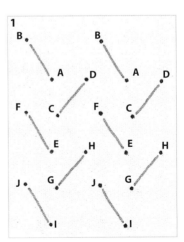

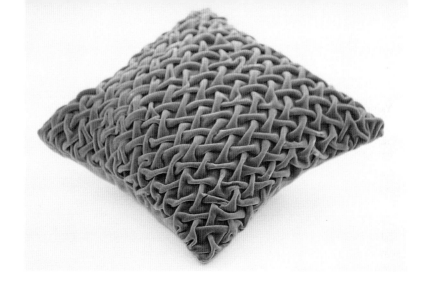

If using velvet, experiment with the direction of the nap. The results of the design vary depending on whether you stitch with or against the nap.

Move to C, keeping the thread slack between A/B and C. Pick up the dots at C and D, bringing them together before moving on to E. Continue down the length of the grid. Then work the second row, repeating across the width of the grid.

When all the smocking is complete, pin the muslin to the wrong side of the pillow front. Baste around the edges along the seam allowance.

**To assemble the pillow**
With right sides together, sew the pillow front to the back, leaving an opening.

Insert the pillow form and slipstitch the opening closed.

# resources

## Yarns

Yarn Barn
930 Massachusetts
Lawrence, Kansas 66044
www.yarnbarn-ks.com

Sally Houk Exclusives
50 Grand Boulevard
Shelby, Ohio 44875
www.picturetrail.com/sallyhouke
xclusives

Fibers Etc.
705 Court C
Tacoma, WA 98402
(253) 531-3257/(253) 572-1859

## Fabrics–Retail

Satin Moon Fabrics
32 Clement Street
San Francisco, CA 94118
Fabrics, Tassels, Ribbons

Sarah's Fabrics
925 Massachusetts Street
Lawrence, KS 66044
Fabrics, Ribbons

Joe's Fabric Warehouse
102 Orchard Street
New York, NY 10002
Discount decorator fabric

Ah! Kimono
16004 NE 195th Street
Woodinville, WA 98072
www.ahkimono.com
Kimono yardage

Hands of the Hills
3016 78th Avenue SE
Mercer Island, WA 98040
www.handsofthehills.com
Thai and Burmese fabrics

Calico Corners
6617 W. 119th Street
Overland Park, KS 66209
www.calicocorners.com

## Fabrics available through architects and interior designers

Brunschwig & Fils
www.brunschwig.com

Scalamandre
www.scalamandre.com

Stroheim & Romann
www.stroheim.com

## Down Pillow Forms

ABC Carpet & Home
888 Broadway
New York, NY 10003
www.ABChome.com

Haberman Fabrics
905 South Main St.
Royal Oak, MI 48067
www.habermanfabrics.com

## Notions

Professional Sewing Supplies
P.O. Box 14272
Seattle, WA 98114
Extra Fine Fusing Tape

Sulky of America
3113 Broadpoint Drive
Punta Gorda, FL 33983
www.sulky.com
Decorative thread

On the Surface
P.O. Box 8026
Wilmette, Il 60091
Spinster

Clotilde
P.O. Box 7500
Big Sandy, Tx 75755
www.clotilde.com
Seams Great, Tiger Tape™

Taunton Press
www.taunton.com
Art Stars Embroidery Design
(see page 111)

# acknowledgments

Every once in a while, someone comes along in your life who makes an impact in the way you think and work, and Trisha Malcolm is one of those people for me. I've always admired her fashion instincts, her editorial style and her work ethic; plus, I just plain enjoy her company. I want to thank Trisha for giving me the opportunity to create this book. Art Joinnides made the first phone call. I appreciate his confidence in me, the opportunity to work for him again and that he listened to Trisha. Working with the staff at Sixth&Spring Books has been a real pleasure. Michelle Lo organized all aspects of this book and managed to keep me on task, assemble the many players and coordinate all of the materials. I am thrilled with the art direction of Chi Ling Moy and her immediate and clear insight into how this book should look. Without the beautiful illustrations of Phoebe Gaughan, this book wouldn't be as lovely as it is. I also extend my gratitude to Pat Harste for editing my instructions for consistency and clarity. And of course, no book of mine feels right without the incredible photography of Jack Deutsch. He and his assistant, Gene Mozgalevsky make it so easy to "see," and I trust their sense of style and taste and their ability to lead me to the obvious conclusion. My staff in Topeka is always there for me. I lean on Kathy Davis continually for her perfect instincts and impeccable sewing. Erin Snethen pitches in to help develop design concepts and Glenda Printz organizes my life in order to leave me free to create. Sewing has been my passion for as long as I can remember, thanks to my mother closing her eyes and letting me use her precious sewing machine when I was way too young to operate it properly.